OECD Skills Studies

The Survey of Adult Skills

READER'S COMPANION
SECOND EDITION

OECD
BETTER POLICIES FOR BETTER LIVES

This work is published under the responsibility of the Secretary-General of the OECD. The opinions expressed and arguments employed herein do not necessarily reflect the official views of the OECD member countries.

This document and any map included herein are without prejudice to the status of or sovereignty over any territory, to the delimitation of international frontiers and boundaries and to the name of any territory, city or area.

Please cite this publication as:
OECD (2016), *The Survey of Adult Skills: Reader's Companion, Second Edition*, OECD Skills Studies, OECD Publishing, Paris.
http://dx.doi.org/10.1787/9789264258075-en

ISBN 978-92-64-25806-8 (print)
ISBN 978-92-64-25807-5 (PDF)

Series: OECD Skills Studies
ISSN 2307-8723 (print)
ISSN 2307-8731 (online)

The statistical data for Israel are supplied by and under the responsibility of the relevant Israeli authorities. The use of such data by the OECD is without prejudice to the status of the Golan Heights, East Jerusalem and Israeli settlements in the West Bank under the terms of international law.

Photo credits:
© aleksandr-mansurov-ru/iStockphoto
© Dmitry_Tsvetkov/Shutterstock.com
© Don Pablo/Shutterstock
© Jamie Grill/Getty Images
© Jaroslav Machacek/Shutterstock
© Konstantin Chagin/Shutterstock
© Lightspring/Shutterstock
© momentimages/Tetra Images/Inmagine LTD
© Monty Rakusen/cultura/Corbis
© Ocean/Corbis
© Rob Lewine/Getty Images

Corrigenda to OECD publications may be found on line at: *www.oecd.org/about/publishing/corrigenda.htm*.

Foreword

In a world in which millions of people are unemployed while many employers complain that they cannot find qualified workers something is obviously out of balance. One of those issues is the match between the supply of and demand for skills. Governments need a clearer picture, not only of how labour markets are changing, but of how well-equipped their citizens are to participate in, and benefit from, increasingly knowledge-based economies. The Survey of Adult Skills, a product of the OECD Programme for the International Assessment of Adult Competencies (PIAAC), is providing that picture. It captures information about adults' proficiency in literacy, numeracy and problem-solving skills, and whether and how those skills are used on the job and throughout life.

Skills Matter: Further Results from the Survey of Adult Skills expands on the data and analysis examined in the *OECD Skills Outlook 2013: First Results from the Survey of Adult Skills* by including data from nine additional countries that conducted the survey in 2014-15. The results show that poor skills severely limit people's access to better-paying and more rewarding jobs. The distribution of skills also has significant implications for how the benefits of economic growth are shared within societies. Put simply, where large shares of adults have poor skills, it becomes difficult to introduce productivity-enhancing technologies and new ways of working, which in turn stalls improvements in living standards. Importantly, the results show that skills affect more than earnings and employment. In all countries, adults with lower skills are far more likely than those with better literacy skills to report poor health, to perceive themselves as objects rather than actors in political processes, and to have less trust in others.

The report also finds that acquiring relevant skills is certainly key, but may not be enough to integrate successfully in the labour market. Skills must be used productively, not only to keep them from atrophying, but also to reap some of the intangible benefits of skills proficiency that contribute to adults' general well-being. For example, this report shows that the intensity with which workers use their information-processing skills in their jobs is related to the likelihood of being satisfied at work.

Going forward, the OECD is working with governments to develop national skills strategies that ensure that their citizens are equipped with the right skills for 21st-century economies and use those skills productively. We know that skills matter for both workers and employers; now it's time to get the balance right.

Angel Gurría
OECD Secretary-General

Acknowledgements

The Survey of Adult Skills is a collaborative endeavour involving the participating countries, the OECD Secretariat, the European Commission and an international Consortium led by Educational Testing Service (ETS). This report was prepared by William Thorn, with the assistance of Vanessa Denis and Ji Eun Chung. Marilyn Achiron, Marika Boiron, Jennifer Cannon, Cassandra Davis and Marta Encinas-Martin provided valuable support in the editorial and production process. Administrative assistance was provided by Sabrina Leonarduzzi.

The international Consortium was responsible for developing the assessment instruments and preparing the underlying data under the direction of Irwin Kirsch.

The development and implementation of the project was steered by the PIAAC Board of Participating Countries. During the implementation of the 2nd Round of the Survey of Adult Skills (2011 to 2016), the Board was chaired by Aviana Bulgarelli (Italy) from 2016, Patrick Bussière (Canada) from 2014 to 2015 and Dan McGrath (United States) from 2010 to 2016. A full list of the members of the Board together with the names of the National Project Managers, experts, members of the international Consortium and staff of the OECD Secretariat who have contributed to the project can be found in Annexes C and D.

Table of Contents

INTRODUCTION 13

CHAPTER 1 **WHAT THE SURVEY OF ADULT SKILLS (PIAAC) MEASURES** 15

Some major features of the assessment 16
- An assessment of key information-processing competencies 16
- A use-oriented conception of competency 16
- Proficiency as a continuum 16
- The importance of contextual information 17

An overview of literacy, numeracy and problem solving in technology-rich environments ... 17

Literacy 19
- Definition 19
- Content 19
- Cognitive strategies 19
- Contexts 20
- Distribution of test items by task characteristics 20
- Literacy sample items 21
- Reading components 23
- Examples of reading component items 23

Numeracy 24
- Definition 24
- Content 24
- Representations of mathematical information 24
- Cognitive strategies 25
- Contexts 25
- Distribution of test items by task characteristics 26
- Numeracy sample items 26

Problem solving in technology-rich environments 28
- Definition 28
- Content 29
- Cognitive strategies 29
- Contexts 29
- Distribution of test items by task characteristics 29
- Problem-solving sample item 31

CHAPTER 2 **THE BACKGROUND QUESTIONNAIRE OF THE SURVEY OF ADULT SKILLS (PIAAC)** ... 35

The characteristics and background of respondents 36

Educational attainment and participation in learning activities 37

Labour force status, work history and job characteristics 37

Social participation and health 38

The use of skills 38
- Engagement as a component of proficiency 39
- The role of literacy and numeracy practices and computer use in maintaining and developing skills ... 39
- Comparative information on a broader range of key skills 39
- Demand for skills 39
- Skills use: Task clusters 39

CHAPTER 3 **THE METHODOLOGY OF THE SURVEY OF ADULT SKILLS (PIAAC) AND THE QUALITY OF DATA**............45

Assessment design..47
- Pathways through the cognitive assessments in the Survey of Adult Skills (PIAAC): Computer-based assessment........48

Sampling..50
- The target population and sampling frame..51
- Coverage of the target population...53
- Sample size...53
- Sample design..54

Translation and adaptation of instruments..54

Survey administration..54

Response rates and non-response bias analysis...55

Literacy-related non-response..58

Scoring...59

Overall assessment of data quality..60

CHAPTER 4 **REPORTING THE RESULTS OF THE SURVEY OF ADULT SKILLS (PIAAC)**..........................63

The proficiency scales..64

Proficiency levels..64
- Literacy and numeracy..71
- Problem solving in technology-rich environments..73
- A note about the reporting of problem solving in technology-rich environments.........74

Test languages and reporting...75

CHAPTER 5 **RELATIONSHIP OF THE SURVEY OF ADULT SKILLS (PIAAC) TO OTHER INTERNATIONAL SKILLS SURVEYS**..77

Countries and economies participating in the Survey of Adult Skills (PIAAC) and IALS and/or ALL............78

Constructs and instruments: The Survey of Adult Skills, ALL and IALS................................79
- Literacy...79
- Numeracy..79
- Problem solving in technology-rich environments..80
- Mode of delivery...80

Comparability of background questions..80

Survey methods and operational standards and procedures..80
- The target population...81
- Sample design..81
- Survey operations...81
- Survey response..82

Educational attainment in IALS..82

Summary of the relationship between the Survey of Adult Skills (PIAAC), IALS and ALL......82

The relationship between the Survey of Adult Skills (PIAAC), LAMP and STEP...................82
- LAMP..83
- STEP...83

CHAPTER 6 **RELATIONSHIP BETWEEN THE SURVEY OF ADULT SKILLS (PIAAC) AND THE OECD PROGRAMME FOR INTERNATIONAL STUDENT ASSESSMENT (PISA)**..87

PISA cohorts in the target population of the Survey of Adult Skills (PIAAC)........................88

Differences in the target populations...88

Skills assessed..88

Psychometric links...89

The relationships between constructs in the domains of literacy, numeracy and problem solving 89
- Literacy 89
- Numeracy 91
- Problem solving 92

Conclusion 93

CHAPTER 7 **THE SURVEY OF ADULT SKILLS (PIAAC) AND "KEY COMPETENCIES"** 95

The definition of key competencies 96
- What is competency? 96
- What is a key competency or skill? 96

The Survey of Adult Skills (PIAAC) and key competencies 98

CHAPTER 8 **THE SURVEY OF ADULT SKILLS (PIAAC) AND THE MEASUREMENT OF HUMAN CAPITAL** 101

Defining "human capital" 102

Coverage of the dimensions of human capital in the Survey of Adult Skills (PIAAC) 102

Educational attainment as a measure of human capital 104

Comparing measures of human capital 105

Empirical evidence 105

Enhancing the measurement of human capital 106

ANNEX A **RELATIONSHIP BETWEEN THE LEVEL OF DESCRIPTORS USED IN THE SURVEY OF ADULT SKILLS (PIAAC) AND OTHER SKILLS SURVEYS** 109

ANNEX B **CONTENT OF BACKGROUND QUESTIONNAIRES IN THE SURVEY OF ADULT SKILLS (PIAAC) AND OTHER SKILLS SURVEYS** 115

ANNEX C **PROJECT PARTICIPANTS IN ROUND 1 OF THE SURVEY OF ADULT SKILLS** 117

ANNEX D **PROJECT PARTICIPANTS IN ROUND 2 OF THE SURVEY OF ADULT SKILLS** 123

BOXES

Box 1.1 Competencies or skills? 17

Box 2.1 Using Item Response Theory to derive skills use indicators in the Survey of Adults Skills (PIAAC).................. 41

Box 2.2 Deriving the survey's measures of skills mismatch in literacy, numeracy or problem solving 43

Box 3.1 How the Survey of Adult Skills (PIAAC) was managed.. 47

FIGURE

Figure 3.1 Pathways through the cognitive assessments in the Survey of Adult Skills (PIAAC): Computer-based assessment 48

TABLES

Table 1.1 Summary of assessment domains in the Survey of Adult Skills (PIAAC) 18

Table 1.2 Distribution of literacy items by medium 20

Table 1.3 Distribution of literacy items by context 20

Table 1.4 Distribution of literacy items by cognitive strategy 20

Table 1.5 Distribution of numeracy items by response type 26

Table 1.6 Distribution of numeracy items by context 26

Table 1.7 Distribution of numeracy items by mathematical content 26

Table 1.8 Distribution of problem-solving tasks by cognitive dimensions 30

Table 1.9 Distribution of problem-solving tasks by technology dimensions 30

Table 1.10 Distribution of problem-solving tasks by context... 30

Table 1.11 Distribution of problem-solving tasks by intrinsic complexity (number of steps) 30

Table 1.12 Distribution of problem-solving tasks by intrinsic complexity (number of constraints) 30

Table 1.13 Distribution of problem-solving tasks by explicitness of problem statement 30

Table 2.1 Data collected concerning the characteristics and background of respondents 36

Table 2.2 Information collected regarding educational experience and current participation in learning activities........... 37

Table 2.3 Information collected regarding labour force status, work history and job characteristics........................ 38

Table 2.4 Information collected on social participation and health.. 38

Table 2.5 Information collected regarding tasks and activities in work and everyday life...................................... 40

Table 2.6 Skills use indicators 41

Table 2.7 Information collected on aspects of qualifications and skills match/mismatch 42

Table 3.1 List of participating countries and economies and dates of key phases.. 46

Table 3.2 Areas of activity covered by the PIAAC Standards and Guidelines 46

Table 3.3 Participation in the cognitive-assessment modules 49

Table 3.4 Sampling frames for countries/economies with registry samples 50

Table 3.5 Sampling frames for countries/economies using master samples 54

Table 3.6 Sampling frames for countries/economies using area samples 51

Table 3.7 Exclusions from target population 52

Table 3.8 Sample size 53

Table 3.9 Achieved response rates and population coverage 56

Table 3.10 PIAAC NRBA outcome summary for countries/economies with response rates less than 70% 57

Table 3.11 Literacy-related non-response to the assessment: Proportion of respondents 58

Table 3.12 Scoring of paper-based instruments: Within- and between-country agreement.................................... 59

Table 4.1 Probability of successfully completing items of varying difficulty for a person scoring 300 on the literacy scale................... 64

Table 4.2 Literacy item map.. 65

Table 4.3 Numeracy item map.. 67

Table 4.4   Problem solving in technology-rich environments item map 69

Table 4.5   Proficiency levels: Literacy and numeracy 71

Table 4.6   Probability of successfully completing items at different difficulty levels, by proficiency score: Literacy 72

Table 4.7   Probability of successfully completing items at different difficulty levels, by proficiency score: Numeracy 72

Table 4.8   Technology, task and cognitive features of problems at each of the three main levels of proficiency 73

Table 4.9   Proficiency levels: Problem solving in technology-rich environments 73

Table 4.10   Probability of successfully completing items at different difficulty levels by proficiency score: Problem solving
            in technology-rich environments 74

Table 4.11   Test languages by country 75

Table 5.1   Countries and economies participating in IALS, ALL and PIAAC: Dates of data collection 78

Table 5.2   Skills assessed in the Survey of Adult Skills (PIAAC), ALL and IALS 79

Table 5.3   Population coverage: IALS, ALL and the Survey of Adult Skills (PIAAC) 81

Table 5.4   Response rates: IALS, ALL and the Survey of Adult Skills (PIAAC) 82

Table 5.5   Skills assessed in the Survey of Adult Skills (PIAAC), STEP, LAMP, ALL and IALS 83

Table 6.1   Age of PISA cohorts in 2011-12 and 2014-15 88

Table 6.2   Comparison of the Survey of Adult Skills (PIAAC) and PISA: Skills assessed 89

Table 6.3   Comparison of the Survey of Adult Skills (PIAAC) and PISA: Literacy 90

Table 6.4   Comparison of the Survey of Adult Skills (PIAAC) and PISA: Numeracy 91

Table 6.5   Comparison of the Survey of Adult Skills (PIAAC) and PISA: Problem solving 93

Table 7.1   Competency groups and examples of specific competencies in competency frameworks 97

Table 7.2   Key competencies and skills covered in the Survey of Adult Skills (PIAAC) 98

Table 8.1   Components of human capital 102

Table 8.2   Coverage of the dimensions of human capital directly assessed in the Survey of Adult Skills (PIAAC) 103

Table 8.3   Coverage of the dimensions of human capital by educational qualifications 104

Table 8.4   Comparison of direct measures from the Survey of Adult Skills (PIAAC) and qualifications on four criteria 105

Table A.1   Location of items on the literacy scale using RP67 and RP80 110

Table A.2   Location of items on the numeracy scale using RP67 and RP80 112

Table A.3   Descriptors of literacy proficiency levels 113

Table A.4   Descriptors of literacy proficiency levels 114

Table B.1   Summary of the background variables common to the Survey of Adult Skills (PIAAC), IALS and ALL 116

Follow OECD Publications on:

 http://twitter.com/OECD_Pubs

 http://www.facebook.com/OECDPublications

 http://www.linkedin.com/groups/OECD-Publications-4645871

 http://www.youtube.com/oecdilibrary

 http://www.oecd.org/oecddirect/

Introduction

This companion volume to the international reports presenting results for the Survey of Adult Skills (PIAAC) (OECD, 2013 and 2016) offers an overview of the "what" and "how" of the Survey of Adult Skills, a product of the Programme for the International Assessment of Adult Competencies, or PIAAC. Its primary objective is to help readers to understand and interpret the results from the survey. To this end, it explains, in a non-technical way, the methodologies underpinning the design of the Survey of Adult Skills (PIAAC) and operational aspects of the survey, such as sampling, data collection and response rates, and how results are reported.

To date, two 'rounds' of the survey have been undertaken. The first, which collected data in 2011-12 involved 24 countries/economies. The second, which collected data in 2014-15 involved a further nine countries/economies. The countries participating in Round 1 were: Australia, Austria, Belgium, Canada, the Czech Republic, Cyprus,[1] Denmark, Estonia, Finland, France, Germany, Ireland, Italy, Japan, Korea, the Netherlands, Norway, Poland, the Russian Federation, the Slovak Republic, Spain, Sweden, the United Kingdom and the United States. In Belgium, data was collected in the Flanders region only. In the United Kingdom, two of the four devolved administrations participated in the survey: England and Northern Ireland. In Round 2 of the survey, the participating countries were: Chile, Greece, Indonesia, Israel, Lithuania, New Zealand, Singapore, Slovenia and Turkey.[2] In Indonesia, data was collected only in the Jakarta municipal area.

A more detailed and technically oriented presentation of the survey, the methodologies used, and the quality of the data output can be found in the *Technical Report of the Survey of Adult Skills, Second Edition* (OECD, forthcoming).

The report addresses four topics:

- what is measured by the Survey of Adult Skills
- how the survey was designed and implemented
- how the results from the survey are reported
- how the survey is related to previous adult skills surveys, to the OECD Programme for International Student Assessment (PISA), and to work on measuring key competencies and human capital.

WHAT IS MEASURED?

Chapter 1 describes the survey's approach to assessing key information-processing skills. In particular, it presents the main elements of the conceptual frameworks defining the constructs of literacy, numeracy and problem solving in technology-rich environments measured by the survey. The Survey of Adult Skills (PIAAC) is designed not only to provide valid and reliable estimates of the competency of the adult population in key information-processing skills, but also to identify differences in proficiency between population sub-groups, to better understand how such skills are developed, maintained and used, and to determine the impact of different levels of proficiency on life chances. Chapter 2 describes the content of the background questionnaire and the rationale behind its design.

ASPECTS OF THE DESIGN AND IMPLEMENTATION OF THE SURVEY

In order to interpret the results from the Survey of Adult Skills, it is essential to understand not only what was measured but how the survey was designed and implemented. Chapter 3 presents the key aspects of the survey's design, describes how the survey was implemented, and provides an overview of the quality of the resulting data.

HOW RESULTS ARE REPORTED

What does it mean to have a particular proficiency score or to be described as having a particular level of proficiency in literacy, numeracy or problem solving in technology-rich environments? Chapter 4 describes how the results from the survey are reported, with an emphasis on the meaning of the scores and proficiency levels.

HOW THE SURVEY RELATES TO OTHER WORK ON MEASURING AND ASSESSING SKILLS AND HUMAN CAPITAL

The Survey of Adult Skills (PIAAC) does not exist in isolation; understanding how the survey relates to other international surveys of adult literacy and how it relates to the OECD assessment of 15-year-old students (the Programme for International Student Assessment or PISA) is important for interpreting its results. To what extent do these surveys assess the same skills? How should similarities and differences in results be interpreted? Similarly, it is important to understand how the survey relates to the concept of "competency" and to the evolution of the definition of "key" or "essential" skills and competencies that has occurred since the 1980s, as well as to debates about measuring human capital. Chapter 5 describes the links between the Survey of Adult Skills and other international adult skills surveys. The relationship between the survey and PISA is discussed in Chapter 6. Chapter 7 explores the relationship between the survey and competency frameworks. The extent to which direct measures of skills should be seen as an alternative or complement to traditional indicators of human capital is addressed in Chapter 8.

Notes

1. *Note by Turkey:* The information in this document with reference to "Cyprus" relates to the southern part of the Island. There is no single authority representing both Turkish and Greek Cypriot people on the Island. Turkey recognises the Turkish Republic of Northern Cyprus (TRNC). Until a lasting and equitable solution is found within the context of the United Nations, Turkey shall preserve its position concerning the "Cyprus issue".

Note by all the European Union Member States of the OECD and the European Union: The Republic of Cyprus is recognised by all members of the United Nations with the exception of Turkey. The information in this document relates to the area under the effective control of the Government of the Republic of Cyprus.

2. The names of the countries participating in Round 2 of the Survey of Adult Skills are presented in blue in all figures and tables.

References

OECD (forthcoming), *Technical Report of the Survey of Adult Skills, Second Edition*.

OECD (2016), *Skills Matter: Further Results from the Survey of Adult Skills*, OECD Skills Studies, OECD Publishing, Paris, http://dx.doi. org/10.1787/ 9789264258051-en.

OECD (2013), *OECD Skills Outlook 2013: First Results from the Survey of Adult Skills*, OECD Publishing, Paris, http://dx.doi.org/ 10.1787/ 9789264204256-en.

What the Survey of Adult Skills (PIAAC) measures

This chapter describes the approach used by the Survey of Adult Skills (PIAAC) and some of the key features of the survey. It then discusses the content, cognitive processes and contexts applicable to the three domains assessed: literacy, numeracy and problem solving in technology-rich environments. Sample items are also provided.

The Survey of Adult Skills (PIAAC) assesses the proficiency of adults in three information-processing skills essential for full participation in the knowledge-based economies and societies of the 21st century: literacy, numeracy and problem solving in technology-rich environments. This chapter describes the constructs measured in the survey and the information sought regarding skills use and the characteristics of respondents. First, a general description of the survey's approach to assessing adult skills is provided.

SOME MAJOR FEATURES OF THE ASSESSMENT

An assessment of key information-processing competencies

The skills assessed in the Survey of Adult Skills are conceived as "key information-processing competencies".[1] They represent skills essential for accessing, understanding, analysing and using text-based information and, in the case of some mathematical information, information in the form of representations (e.g. pictures, graphs). These texts and representations may exist in the form of printed material or screen-based displays.

They are considered to be "key information-processing skills" in that they are:

- Necessary for fully integrating and participating in the labour market, education and training, and social and civic life.
- Highly transferable, in that they are relevant to many social contexts and work situations.
- "Learnable" and, therefore, subject to the influence of policy.

At the most fundamental level, literacy and numeracy constitute a foundation for developing higher-order cognitive skills, such as analytic reasoning, and are essential for gaining access to and understanding specific domains of knowledge. In addition, these skills are relevant across the range of life contexts, from education through work to home life and interaction with public authorities. In information-rich societies, in which information in text format (whether print-based or digital) is ubiquitous, a capacity to read and respond to text-based information is essential, whether that means understanding the user information on a packet of medicine, reacting appropriately to a memo from a colleague or superior at work, or enrolling a child at school. Similarly, numeracy skills are essential in most areas of life, from buying and selling goods, to understanding pension entitlements, to planning one's working day.

In addition, the capacity to manage information and solve problems in technology-rich environments – that is, to access, evaluate, analyse and communicate information – is becoming as important as understanding and interpreting text-based information and being able to handle mathematical content. Information and communication technology (ICT) applications have become a feature in most workplaces, in education, and in everyday life.

A use-oriented conception of competency

Literacy, numeracy and problem solving are competencies that are essential for functioning in the modern world, for realising the myriad tasks adults must undertake in the various life contexts. Adults read, deal with situations involving mathematical content and representations, and try to solve problems in order to do things and achieve certain objectives in a range of contexts. Consequently, the focus of the Survey of Adult Skills is less on the mastery of certain content (e.g. vocabulary or arithmetical operations) and a set of cognitive strategies than on the ability to draw on this content and these strategies to successfully perform information-processing tasks in a variety of real-world situations.

Proficiency as a continuum

The competencies assessed in the Survey of Adult Skills are understood as involving a continuum of proficiency. Individuals are considered to be proficient to a greater or a lesser degree in the competency in question as opposed to being either "proficient" or "not proficient". In other words, there is no threshold that separates those who have the competency in question from those who do not. The measurement scales describe gradations in the complexity of the information-processing tasks in the domains of literacy, numeracy and problem solving in technology-rich environments. In each domain, this complexity is seen as a function of a small number of factors, such as the type of cognitive operations required by the task, the presence of distracting information, and the nature of information and knowledge required to successfully complete a task.

At the lower end of the proficiency scale, individuals have skills that allow them to undertake tasks of limited complexity, such as locating single pieces of information in short texts in the absence of other distracting information, or performing simple mathematical operations involving a single step, such as counting or ordering. At the highest level of proficiency, adults can undertake tasks that involve integrating information across multiple dense texts, reasoning by inference, working with mathematical arguments and models, and solving complex problems using information technologies that require navigation and the use of multiple tools.

Literacy and numeracy are often described as "basic" skills, in that they provide a "foundation" on which the development of other competencies rests. This description is unfortunate in that it can give the impression that such skills are less complex than certain other "higher-order" skills, or that the policy interest in such skills lies in ensuring that the population possesses an acceptable minimum or basic level of proficiency in these skills. It is important to emphasise that the objective of the Survey of Adult Skills is to see how the adult population is distributed over the entire spectrum of proficiency in each of the domains assessed, not to assess whether adults have achieved a basic level of skills.

The importance of contextual information

In addition to estimating the level and distribution of proficiency in the population, the Survey of Adult Skills seeks to provide information that will enable policy makers and others to better understand the relationship between the measured skills and economic and social outcomes, and the factors related to acquiring, maintaining, developing and losing skills. The assessment of literacy, numeracy and problem solving in technology-rich environments is, thus, complemented by information on the use of the measured cognitive skills and certain generic skills (see Chapter 2 for more information). This information includes details about respondents' literacy and numeracy practices and their use of information and communication technologies (ICT) at work and in other contexts. It also encompasses the extent to which individuals are required to use a range of generic skills in their work, including interpersonal skills, such as collaboration and influencing, learning skills, organising, including both self-organisation and delegating tasks, and physical skills. Respondents also report on how and whether their skills and qualifications match the requirements of their jobs.

Box 1.1 **Competencies or skills?**

A distinction is sometimes made between "competency" and "skill" in the literature on education and training. Competency is often presented as a capacity that can be applied to a relatively wide range of "real" contexts, while "skill" is considered a constituent unit of competency, that is, a specific capacity, often technical in nature, relevant to a specific context. For example, competency has been defined as "a combination of knowledge, skills and attitudes appropriate to the context" (European Commission, 2007). In the context of the Survey of Adult Skills (PIAAC), however, no attempt is made to differentiate competency and skill, and the terms are used interchangeably in this report. Both terms refer to the ability or capacity of an agent to act appropriately in a given situation. Both involve the application of knowledge (explicit and/or tacit), the use of tools, cognitive and practical strategies and routines, and both imply beliefs, dispositions and values (e.g. attitudes). In addition, neither competency nor skill is conceived as being related to any particular context of performance, nor is a skill regarded as one of the atomic units that combine to form competency. Skills (competencies) can always be broken down into smaller and more specific skills (or competencies) or aggregated into more general skills (or competencies). This question is also discussed in Chapter 7.

AN OVERVIEW OF LITERACY, NUMERACY AND PROBLEM SOLVING IN TECHNOLOGY-RICH ENVIRONMENTS

Groups of experts in their fields developed the frameworks for each of the skills domains assessed in the Survey of Adult Skills. They guided the development and selection of assessment items and the interpretation of results. Their work is presented in *Literacy, Numeracy and Problem Solving in Technology-Rich Environments: Framework for the Survey of Adult Skills* (OECD, 2012).[2] The frameworks define and describe what is measured. In each case, three main dimensions are identified:

- Content – the artefacts, tools, knowledge, representations and cognitive challenges that constitute the corpus adults must respond to or use.

- Cognitive strategies – the processes that adults must bring into play to respond to or use given content in an appropriate manner.

- Context – the different situations in which adults have to read, display numerate behaviour, and solve problems.

Table 1.1 provides an overview of each of the three domains, including a definition and the content, cognitive strategies and contexts related to each. These are described in more detail in the remainder of this chapter.

Table 1.1 Summary of assessment domains in the Survey of Adult Skills (PIAAC)

	Literacy	Numeracy	Problem solving in technology-rich environments
Definition	Literacy is defined as the ability to understand, evaluate, use and engage with *written texts* to participate in society, to achieve one's goals, and to develop one's knowledge and potential. Literacy encompasses a range of skills from the decoding of written words and sentences to the comprehension, interpretation, and evaluation of complex texts. It does not, however, involve the production of text (writing[1]). Information on the skills of adults with low levels of proficiency is provided by an assessment of reading components that covers text vocabulary, sentence comprehension and passage fluency.	Numeracy is defined as the ability to access, use, interpret and communicate mathematical information and ideas in order to engage in and manage the mathematical demands of a range of situations in adult life. To this end, numeracy involves managing a situation or solving a problem in a real context, by responding to mathematical content/information/ideas represented in multiple ways.	Problem solving in technology-rich environments is defined as the ability to use digital technology, communication tools and networks to acquire and evaluate information, communicate with others and perform practical tasks. The assessment focuses on the abilities to solve problems for personal, work and civic purposes by setting up appropriate goals and plans, and accessing and making use of information through computers and computer networks.
Content	Different types of text. Texts are characterised by their medium (print-based or digital) and by their format: ■ Continuous or prose texts ■ Non-continuous or document texts ■ Mixed texts ■ Multiple texts	Mathematical content, information and ideas: ■ Quantity and number ■ Dimension and shape ■ Pattern, relationships and change ■ Data and chance Representations of mathematical information: ■ Objects and pictures ■ Numbers and symbols ■ Visual displays (e.g. diagrams, maps, graphs, tables) ■ Texts ■ Technology-based displays	Technology: ■ Hardware devices ■ Software applications ■ Commands and functions ■ Representations (e.g. text, graphics, video) Tasks: ■ Intrinsic complexity ■ Explicitness of the problem statement
Cognitive strategies	■ Access and identify ■ Integrate and interpret (relating parts of text to one another) ■ Evaluate and reflect	■ Identify, locate or access ■ Act upon and use (order, count, estimate, compute, measure, model) ■ Interpret, evaluate and analyse ■ Communicate	■ Set goals and monitor progress ■ Plan ■ Acquire and evaluate information ■ Use information
Contexts	■ Work-related ■ Personal ■ Society and community ■ Education and training	■ Work-related ■ Personal ■ Society and community ■ Education and training	■ Work-related ■ Personal ■ Society and community

1. The dimension of writing is, however, not part of what the Survey of Adult Skills measures, which is mainly due to the difficulty of assessing writing in a reliable and valid way in an international comparative assessment.

LITERACY

Definition

In the Survey of Adult Skills, literacy is defined as "understanding, evaluating, using and engaging with written texts to participate in society, to achieve one's goals, and to develop one's knowledge and potential".

Key to this definition is the fact that literacy is defined in terms of the *reading* of *written text*s and does not involve either the comprehension or production of spoken language or the production of text (writing). While literacy is commonly seen as encompassing the ability to write as well as read (UNESCO, 2005), the dimension of writing is not part of the construct measured in the Survey of Adult Skills. This is largely because of the difficulty of assessing writing in a reliable and valid way in an international comparative assessment. In addition, literacy is conceived as a skill that involves constructing meaning, and evaluating and using texts to achieve a range of possible goals in a variety of contexts. In other words, in the Survey of Adult Skills, literacy extends well beyond the skills of decoding or comprehending texts to using them appropriately in context.

Content

The corpus of texts to which adults are required to respond are classified along two principle axes: medium and format. Medium refers to the nature of the support in which a text is instantiated or displayed. Format refers to the organisational and structural features of texts, whether digital or print-based.

In terms of *medium*, texts are classified as either digital or print-based. Digital texts are texts that are stored as digital information (a series of 1s and 0s) and accessed in the form of screen-based displays on devices such as computers and smart phones. Print-based texts are texts printed on paper or other material supports; these include newspapers, books, pamphlets and road signs. Digital texts have a range of features, in addition to being displayed on screens, that distinguishes them from print-based texts. These include hypertext links to other documents, specific navigation features (e.g. scroll bars, use of menus) and interactivity. The Survey of Adult Skills is the first international assessment of adult skills to incorporate the reading of digital texts as part of the construct of (reading) literacy.[3]

In terms of *format*, texts are categorised in the following way:

- Continuous texts, which are made up of sentences organised in paragraphs that incorporate a range of rhetorical stances, such as description, narration, instruction and argumentation.
- Non-continuous texts, which are organised in a matrix format or around graphic features. Several different organising structures are identified, including simple and complex lists, graphic documents (e.g. graphs, diagrams), locative documents (e.g. maps) and entry documents (e.g. forms).
- Mixed texts, which involve combinations of continuous and non-continuous elements (e.g. a newspaper article or a webpage that includes text and graphics).
- Multiple texts, which consist of juxtaposing or linking independently generated elements, such as an e-mail that contains a record of the separate messages that constitute an exchange over a period of time, or a blog post that contains an initial text and a string of related texts consisting of comments in response to the initial text and comments in response to other comments.

Cognitive strategies

Readers generally use three broad cognitive strategies when responding to written texts:

- access and identify
- integrate and interpret
- evaluate and reflect.

Accessing and identifying involves locating information in a text. At one extreme, this can be a relatively simple operation when the information sought is clearly identified. At the other, it can be a complicated operation requiring inferential reasoning and an understanding of rhetorical strategies.

Integrating and interpreting involves understanding the relationships between different parts of a text to construct meaning and draw inferences from the text as a whole.

Evaluating and reflecting requires the reader to relate the information in the text to other information, knowledge and experiences, for example, to assess the relevance or credibility of a text.

Contexts

Adults read materials in a variety of contexts that affect the types of texts they encounter, the nature of the content, the motivation to read, and the manner in which texts are interpreted. The texts selected for the literacy assessment are related to four broad contexts:

- work-related
- personal
- society and community
- education and training.

Texts related to *work and occupation* include materials that discuss job search, wages, salaries and other benefits, and the experience of work.

Materials in the area of *personal* include texts concerning the home and family (e.g. interpersonal relationships, personal finances, housing and insurance); health and safety (e.g. drugs and alcohol, disease prevention and treatment, safety and accident prevention, first aid, emergencies, and lifestyle); consumer economics (banking, savings, advertising, prices); and leisure and recreation (travel, recreational activities).

Texts related to *society and community* includes materials that deal with public services, government, community groups and activities, and current events. Materials related to *education and training* cover text which refer to learning opportunities for adults or others.

Distribution of test items by task characteristics

Tables 1.2, 1.3 and 1.4 below show the distribution of the literacy assessment items in the Survey of Adult Skills by task characteristics. The final selection of items was determined taking into account the following factors: the performance of items in the field test, the need to cover the main dimensions of literacy as defined by the assessment frameworks, the need to include sufficient items that had been used in previous surveys to ensure comparability of the results, and the constraints imposed by the assessment design.[4]

Table 1.2 **Distribution of literacy items by medium**

	Final item set	
	Number	**%**
Print-based texts	36	62
Digital texts	22	38
Total	**58**	**100**

Note: Each category includes continuous, non-continuous and combined texts.

Table 1.3 **Distribution of literacy items by context**

	Final item set	
	Number	**%**
Work-related	10	17
Personal	29	50
Society and community	13	23
Education training	6	10
Total	**58**	**100**

Table 1.4 **Distribution of literacy items by cognitive strategy**

	Final item set	
	Number	**%**
Access and identify	32	55
Integrate and interpret	17	29
Evaluate and reflect	9	16
Total	**58**	**100**

Literacy sample items

Two examples of the literacy items used in the Survey of Adult Skills (PIAAC) are presented below. Both use print-based stimuli. The sample problem-solving items presented further below give an idea of the type of "digital" stimulus material used.

The items are presented in the form delivered by the computer-based version of the assessment. To answer the questions, respondents highlighted words and phrases or clicked on the appropriate location on the screen using a mouse.

Sample item 1: Preschool rules

"Preschool Rules" represents an easy item and focuses on the following aspects of the literacy construct:

Medium	Print
Context	Personal
Cognitive strategy	Access and identify

OECD PIAAC

Look at the list of preschool rules. Highlight information in the list to answer the question below.

What is the latest time that children should arrive at preschool?

Preschool Rules

Welcome to our Preschool! We are looking forward to a great year of fun, learning and getting to know each other. Please take a moment to review our preschool rules.

- Please have your child here by 9:00 am.
- Bring a small blanket or pillow and/or a small soft toy for naptime.
- Dress your child comfortably and bring a change of clothing.
- Please no jewelry or candy. If your child has a birthday please talk to your child's teacher about a special snack for the children.
- Please bring your child fully dressed, no pajamas.
- Please sign in with your full signature. This is a licensing regulation. Thank you.
- Breakfast will be served until 7:30 am.
- Medications have to be in original, labeled containers and must be signed into the medication sheet located in each classroom.
- If you have any questions, please talk to your classroom teacher or to Ms. Marlene or Ms. Tree.

Sample items 2 and 3: Physical exercise equipment

In many cases, several questions are associated with the same stimulus material. In the case of the stimulus relating to physical exercise equipment, there are two associated questions or test items.

The first item represents a relatively easy item and focuses on the following aspects of the literacy construct:

Medium	Print
Context	Personal
Cognitive strategy	Access and identify

Respondents answer the question by clicking on the cell in the chart that contains information about exercise equipment. Each of the cells and all of the images can be highlighted by clicking on them and multiple cells can be selected.

PIAAC

Physical Exercise Equipment

Look at the exercise equipment chart. Click on the chart to answer the question below.

Which muscles will benefit most if you use the gym bench?

How to choose?

1. Decide what effect you want the exercise to have on your body.
2. Assess the space you have available at home.
3. Choose the equipment that suits your objectives. If necessary ask a specialist for advice.

For example:

OBJECTIVE	STRATEGY	EQUIPMENT
Burn off calories	Cardiovascular exercises	Rowing machine, Bicycle, Skimachine, Treadmill, Stairs, ….
Strengthen your muscles	Endurance exercises	Bench for Press-ups, Weights and Dumbbells, Elastic Tubes, ….

Effects on…	Cardio-Training					Muscle Building							
	Exercise bicycle	Rowing machine	Stepper	Tread-mill	Air trainer	Dumb-bells, weights	Elastic	Gym bench	Muscle-building bench	Multi-trainer	AB trimmer	AB shaper	AB roller
Arm strength	Ineffective	Good	Average	Ineffective	Good	Very good	Very good	Good	Good	Good	Very good	Good	Good
Leg strength	Good	Very good	Average	Very good	Good	Ineffective	Good	Average	Good	Good	Ineffective	Good	Good
Abdominal muscles	Average	Very good	Good	Good	Average	Ineffective	Good	Very good	Good	Average	Very good	Very good	Very good
Overall muscle building	Ineffective	Very good	Ineffective	Average	Ineffective	Average	Good	Good	Good	Average	Good	Good	Good
Heart/arteries	Very good	Good	Very good	Very good	Good	Ineffective	Average	Average	Average	Good	Average	Average	Average
Flexibility	Ineffective	Good	Ineffective	Ineffective	Average	Average	Average	Good	Ineffective	Ineffective	Average	Good	Good
Joints	Good	Very good	Good	Good	Good	Good	Average	Average	Good	Good	Average	Average	Average
Slimming	Good	Average	Very good	Good	Good	Ineffective	Average	Good	Average	Average	Good	Good	Good
Dangers	None	Back	None	Legs		It is best to learn to use these types of apparatus properly before you make a major effort							

The second item represents a relatively easy item and focuses on the following aspects of the literacy construct:

Medium	Print
Context	Personal
Cognitive strategy	Access and identify

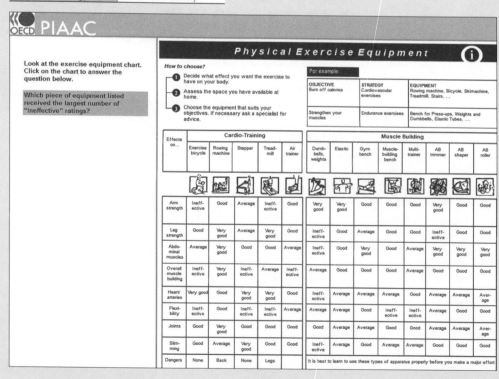

PIAAC — Physical Exercise Equipment

Look at the exercise equipment chart. Click on the chart to answer the question below.

Which piece of equipment listed received the largest number of "Ineffective" ratings?

Reading components

To provide more detailed information about adults with poor literacy skills, the survey's literacy assessment is complemented by a test of "reading components" skills. Reading components are the basic set of decoding skills that are essential for extracting meaning from written texts: knowledge of vocabulary (word recognition), the ability to process meaning at the level of the sentence, and fluency in reading passages of text. Skilled readers are able to undertake these types of operations automatically. To assess this skill, the time taken by respondents to complete the tasks was recorded.

Examples of reading component items

Print vocabulary

Items testing print vocabulary consist of a picture of an object and four printed words, one of which refers to the pictured object. Respondents are asked to circle the word that matches the picture.

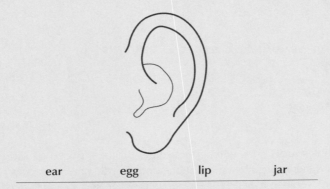

ear	egg	lip	jar

Sentence processing

The sentence-processing items require the respondent to assess whether a sentence makes sense in terms of the properties of the real world or the internal logic of the sentence. The respondent reads the sentence and circles YES if the sentence makes sense, or NO if the sentence does not make sense.

Three girls ate the song.	YES	NO
The man drove the green car.	YES	NO
The lightest balloon floated in the bright sky.	YES	NO
A comfortable pillow is soft and rocky.	YES	NO
A person who is twenty years old is older than a person who is thirty years old.	YES	NO

Passage comprehension

In items assessing passage comprehension, respondents are asked to read a passage in which they are required, at certain points, to select the word from the two alternatives provided that makes the most sense.

To the editor: Yesterday, it was announced that the cost of riding the bus will increase. The price will go up by twenty percent starting next <u>wife / month</u>. As someone who rides the bus every day, I am upset by this <u>foot / increase</u>. I understand that the cost of <u>gasoline / student</u> has risen. I also understand that riders have to pay a fair <u>price / snake</u> for bus service. I am willing to pay a little more because I rely on the bus to get to <u>object / work</u>. But an <u>increase / uncle</u> of twenty percent is too much.

This increase is especially difficult to accept when you see the city's plans to build a new sports stadium. The government will spend millions on this project even though we already have a <u>science / stadium</u>. If we delay the stadium, some of that money can be used to offset the increase in bus <u>fares / views</u>. Then, in a few years, we can decide if we really do need a new sports <u>cloth / arena</u>. Please let the city council know you care about this issue by attending the next public <u>meeting / frames</u>.

NUMERACY

Definition

The Survey of Adult Skills defines numeracy as "the ability to access, use, interpret and communicate mathematical information and ideas, in order to engage in and manage the mathematical demands of a range of situations in adult life" (OECD, 2012). Numeracy is further defined in terms of the concept of "numerate behaviour" that involves managing a situation or solving a problem in a real context by responding to mathematical information and content represented in various ways.

It is recognised that literacy skills such as reading and writing enable numerate behaviour, and that when mathematical representations involve text, performance on numeracy tasks is, in part, dependent on the ability to read and understand text. However, numeracy in the Survey of Adult Skills involves more than applying arithmetical skills to information embedded in text. In particular, numeracy relates to a wide range of skills and knowledge, not just arithmetic knowledge and computation, a range of responses that may involve more than numbers, and responses to a range of representations, not just numbers in texts.

Content

The survey covers four areas of mathematical content, information and ideas:

- quantity and number
- dimension and shape
- pattern, relationships and change
- data and chance.

Quantity encompasses attributes such as the number of features or items, prices, size (e.g. length, area and volume), temperature, humidity, atmospheric pressure, populations and growth rates, revenues and profit, etc. *Number* is fundamental to quantification. Numbers (whether whole numbers or fractions, decimals or percentages) serve as counters or estimators, indicate parts or comparisons. Positive and negative numbers can also serve as directional indicators. In calculations, operations (i.e. the four main operations of $+$, $-$, $\times$, $\div$ and others, such as squaring) are performed on quantities and numbers.

Dimension covers the description of "things" in space, such as projections, lengths, perimeters, areas, planes, surfaces, location, etc. *Shape* involves a category describing real images and entities that can be visualised in two or three dimensions (e.g. houses and buildings, designs in art and craft, safety signs, packaging, snowflakes, knots, crystals, shadows and plants).

Pattern covers regularities encountered in the world, such as those in musical forms, nature, traffic, etc. *Relationships* and *change* relate to the mathematics of how things in the world are associated with one another or develop over time.

Data and chance encompass two separate but related topics. *Data* covers the "big ideas" related to variability, sampling, error, prediction and statistical topics, such as data collection, data displays and graphs. *Chance* covers the "big ideas" related to probability and relevant statistical methods.

Representations of mathematical information

In the Survey of Adult Skills, mathematical information may be represented in the form of:

- objects and pictures
- numbers and symbols
- visual displays; texts
- technology-based displays.

Objects (physical entities) can be counted and measured. *Pictures* (e.g. photographs, paintings, videos) also represent mathematical information such as number, size, volume or location. *Numbers and symbols* include numerals, letters, and operation or relationship signs and formulae. *Visual displays* cover graphic presentations of mathematical information, such as diagrams or charts, graphs and tables (used to display aggregate statistical or quantitative information through objects, counting data, etc.) or maps (e.g. of a city or a project plan). Two different kinds of *text* may be encountered in numeracy tasks. The first involves representing mathematical information in textual form, i.e. as words or phrases that carry mathematical meaning. The second involves expressing mathematical information in mathematical notations or symbols (e.g. numbers, plus or minus signs, symbols for units of measure, etc.) that are surrounded by text that provides additional information and context.

Cognitive strategies

Four processes define the dimension of cognitive strategies:

- identify, locate, or access
- act upon or use
- interpret, evaluate/analyse
- communicate.

In virtually all situations, people have to *identify, locate or access* some mathematical information relevant to their purpose or goal. In isolation, this response type often requires a low level of mathematical understanding or the application of simple arithmetic skills. However, this response type is usually combined with the other types of responses listed below.

Acting upon or using involves the use of known mathematical procedures and rules, such as counting and making calculations. It may also call for ordering or sorting, estimating or using various measuring devices, or for using (or developing) a formula that serves as a model of a situation or a process.

Interpretation involves evaluating the meaning and implications of mathematical or statistical information (e.g. a graph showing variation in an exchange rate) and developing an opinion about the information. *Evaluation/analysis* is in part an extension of interpretation. It involves analysing a problem, evaluating the quality of the solution against some criteria or contextual demands and, if necessary, reviewing the interpretation, analysis and evaluation stages.

While defined as a cognitive process forming part of this dimension of the numeracy framework, the ability to *communicate* numerical and mathematical content is not assessed in the Survey of Adult Skills.

Contexts

The items selected for the numeracy assessment are related to four contexts:

- work-related
- personal
- society and community
- education and training.

Representative tasks related to *work situations* include: completing purchase orders; totalling receipts; calculating change; managing schedules, budgets and project resources; using spreadsheets; organising and packing goods of different shapes; completing and interpreting control charts; making and recording measurements; reading blueprints; tracking expenditures; predicting costs; and applying formulas.

Representative tasks related to the context of *personal life* include: handling money and budgets; shopping and managing personal time; planning travel; playing games of chance; understanding sports scoring and statistics; reading maps; and using measurements in home situations, such as cooking, doing home repairs or pursuing hobbies.

Adults need to have an awareness of what is occurring in the *society, the economy and the environment* (e.g. trends in crime, health, wages, pollution), and may have to take part in social events or community action. This requires a capacity to read and interpret quantitative information presented in the media, including statistical messages and graphs. Adults also have to manage a variety of situations, such as raising funds for a football club or interpreting the results of a study on a medical condition.

Competency in numeracy may enable a person to participate in *education and training*, whether for academic purposes or as part of vocational training. In either case, it is important to know some of the more formal aspects of mathematics that involve symbols, rules and formulae and to understand some of the conventions used to apply mathematical rules and principles.

Distribution of test items by task characteristics

Tables 1.5, 1.6 and 1.7 below show the distribution of the numeracy assessment items included in the Survey of Adult Skills by task characteristics. As in the case of literacy, the final selection of items reflected the performance of items in the field test, the need to cover the main dimensions of literacy as defined by the assessment frameworks, the need to include sufficient items that had been used in previous surveys to ensure comparability of the results, and the constraints imposed by the assessment design.

Table 1.5 **Distribution of numeracy items by response type**

	Final item set	
	Number	**%**
Identify, locate or access	3	5
Act upon, use	34	61
Interpret, evaluate/analyse	19	34
Total	**56**	**100**

Table 1.6 **Distribution of numeracy items by context**

	Final item set	
	Number	**%**
Work-related	13	23
Personal	25	45
Society and community	14	25
Education and training	4	7
Total	**56**	**100**

Table 1.7 **Distribution of numeracy items by mathematical content**

	Final item set	
	Number	**%**
Data and chance	12	21
Dimension and shape	16	29
Pattern, relationships and change	15	27
Quantity and number	13	23
Total	**56**	**100**

Numeracy sample items

Sample item 1: Births in the United States

The items are presented in the form delivered by the computer-based version of the assessment. To answer the questions, respondents clicked in the appropriate box or typed figures in the spaces provided.

This item (of medium difficulty) focuses on the following aspects of the numeracy construct:

Content	Data and chance
Process	Interpret, evaluate
Context	Society and community

Respondents were asked to respond by clicking on one or more of the time periods provided in the left pane on the screen.

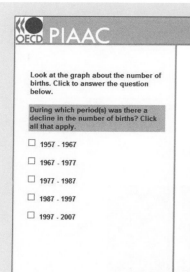

Look at the graph about the number of births. Click to answer the question below.

During which period(s) was there a decline in the number of births? Click all that apply.

☐ 1957 - 1967

☐ 1967 - 1977

☐ 1977 - 1987

☐ 1987 - 1997

☐ 1997 - 2007

The following graph shows the number of births in the United States from 1957 to 2007. Data are presented every 10 years.

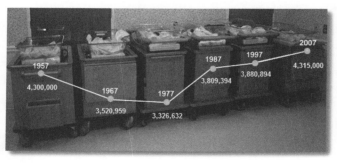

Sample item 2: Thermometer

This item (of low difficulty) focuses on the following aspects of the numeracy construct:

Content	Dimension and shape
Process	Act upon, use (measure)
Context	Personal or work-related

Respondents were asked to type in a numerical response based on the graphic provided.

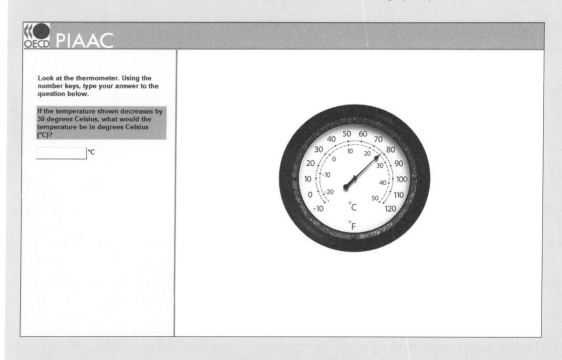

Look at the thermometer. Using the number keys, type your answer to the question below.

If the temperature shown decreases by 30 degrees Celsius, what would the temperature be in degrees Celsius (°C)?

[   ] °C

Sample item 3: Wind power stations

This sample item (of medium difficulty) focuses on the following aspects of the numeracy construct:

Content	Quantity and number
Process	Act upon, use (compute)
Context	Society and community

PIAAC

Wind Power Stations

Read the article about wind power stations. Using the number keys, type your answer to the question below.

How many wind power stations would be needed to replace the power generated by the nuclear reactor?

In 2005, the Swedish government closed the last nuclear reactor at the Barsebäck power plant. The reactor had been generating an average energy output of 3,572 GWh of electrical energy per year.

Work continues in Sweden on installing large offshore wind farms using wind power stations. Each wind power station produces about 6,000 MWh of electrical energy per year.

For your information:
Electrical energy is measured in Watt hours (Wh)

1 kWh	= 1 kilo Wh	=	1,000 Wh
1 MWh	= 1 Mega Wh	=	1,000,000 Wh
1 GWh	= 1 Giga Wh	=	1,000,000,000 Wh

PROBLEM SOLVING IN TECHNOLOGY-RICH ENVIRONMENTS

Definition

In the Survey of Adult Skills, problem solving in technology-rich environments is defined as "using digital technology, communication tools and networks to acquire and evaluate information, communicate with others and perform practical tasks". The first cycle of the Survey of Adult Skills focuses on "the abilities to solve problems for personal, work and civic purposes by setting up appropriate goals and plans, and accessing and making use of information through computers and computer networks" (OECD, 2012).

The problem solving in technology-rich environments domain covers the specific types of problems people deal with when using ICT. These problems share the following characteristics:

- The problem is primarily a consequence of the availability of new technologies.

- The solution to the problem requires the use of computer-based artefacts (applications, representational formats, computational procedures).

- The problems are related to technology-rich environments themselves (e.g. how to operate a computer, how to fix a settings problem, how to use an Internet browser).

Problem solving in technology-rich environments is a domain of competency that represents the intersection of what are sometimes described as "computer literacy" skills (i.e. the capacity to use ICT tools and applications) and the cognitive skills required to solve problems. Some basic knowledge regarding the use of ICT input devices (e.g. use of a keyboard and mouse and screen displays), file management tools, applications (word processing, e-mail), and graphic interfaces is essential for performing assessment tasks. However, the objective is not to test the use of ICT tools and applications in isolation, but rather to assess the capacity of adults to use these tools to access, process, evaluate and analyse information effectively.

Content

The content of the assessment encompasses two areas: technology and tasks.

Technology refers to the devices, applications and functionalities through which problem solving is conducted. It encompasses digital devices such as computers, mobile phones, GPS devices, software applications and the commands, functions and representations of information on which these applications depend. In the first cycle of the survey, only laptop computers with a limited number of simulated software applications – including e-mail, word processing, spreadsheets and websites – were used. For operational reasons, sound, animations and videos were not used.

Tasks are the circumstances that trigger a person's awareness and understanding of the problem and determine the actions needed to be taken in order to solve the problem. Ordinarily, a wide range of conditions can initiate problem solving. Tasks are defined in terms of intrinsic complexity and the explicitness of the problem statement. The *intrinsic complexity* of a problem is determined by:

- the minimum number of steps required to solve the problem
- the number of options or alternatives at various stages in the solution path
- the diversity of operators required to be used, and the complexity of computation/transformation
- the likelihood of impasses or unexpected outcomes
- the number of requirements that have to be satisfied to arrive at a solution
- the amount of transformation required to communicate a solution.

The *explicitness of the problem statement* relates to the extent to which the problem is ill-defined (the task is implicit and its components are largely unspecified) or well-defined (the task is explicit and its components are described in detail).

Cognitive strategies

The process aspect of the assessment relates to the mental structures and processes involved when a person solves a problem. These include setting goals and monitoring progress; planning; locating, selecting and evaluating information; and organising and transforming information.

Setting goals and monitoring progress involves identifying objectives in the context of the constraints (explicit and implicit) of a situation; establishing and applying criteria for respecting constraints and arriving at a solution; monitoring progress; and detecting and interpreting unexpected events, impasses and breakdowns as one proceeds along the path to a solution.

Planning and self-organisation covers the processes of setting up adequate plans, procedures and strategies (operators) and selecting appropriate devices, tools or categories of information.

Acquiring and evaluating information involves orienting and focusing attention; selecting information; assessing the reliability, relevance, adequacy and comprehensibility of information; and reasoning about sources and contents.

Using information involves organising information; integrating information drawn from different and possibly inconsistent texts and from different formats; making informed decisions; transforming information through rewriting, from text to table, from table to graph, etc.; and communicating with relevant parties.

Contexts

The contexts are those of personal life, work-related and society and community.

Distribution of test items by task characteristics

Tables from 1.8 to 1.13 show the distribution of the problem-solving assessment items included in the Survey of Adult Skills by task characteristics.

In total 16 items were administered in the assessment of problem solving in technology environments. Items consisted of scenarios that involved a number of sub-tasks such as searching through simulated websites for relevant information or transferring information from one application to another. The time taken to complete the problem-solving tasks was considerably longer than that in either literacy or numeracy.

Table 1.8 **Distribution of problem-solving tasks by cognitive dimensions**

Dimension	Number[1]
Setting goals and monitoring progress	4
Planning	7
Acquiring and evaluating information	8
Using information	6

1. Does not add up to 16 as some tasks are coded to more than one dimension.

Table 1.9 **Distribution of problem-solving tasks by technology dimensions**

Dimension	Number[1]
Web	7
Spreadsheet	4
E-mail	9

1. Does not add up to 16 as some tasks are coded to more than one dimension.

Table 1.10 **Distribution of problem-solving tasks by context**

Dimension	Number
Personal	8
Work-related	4
Society and community	2

Table 1.11 **Distribution of problem-solving tasks by intrinsic complexity (number of steps)**

Dimension	Number
Single step	8
Multiple steps	6

Table 1.12 **Distribution of problem-solving tasks by intrinsic complexity (number of constraints)**

Dimension	Number
Single constraint	7
Multiple constraints	7

Table 1.13 **Distribution of problem-solving tasks by explicitness of problem statement**

Dimension	Number
Ill-defined problem statement	7
Well-defined problem statement	7

Problem-solving sample item

An example of a problem-solving item is provided below. This item involves a scenario in which the respondent assumes the role of a job-seeker. Respondents access and evaluate information relating to job search in a simulated web environment. This environment includes tools and functionalities similar to those found in real-life applications. Users are able to:

- click on links on both the results page and associated web pages
- navigate, using the back and forward arrows or the Home icon
- bookmark web pages and view or change those bookmarks.

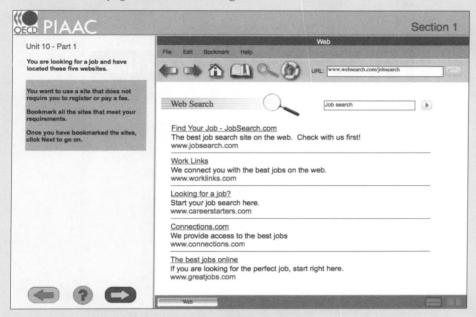

The first stimulus accessed by respondents is the results page of the search-engine application, which lists five employment agency websites. To complete the task successfully, respondents have to search through the pages of the listed websites to identify whether registration or the payment of a fee is required in order to gain further information about available jobs. Respondents can click on the links on the search page to be directed to the websites identified. For example, by clicking on the "Work Links" link, the respondent is directed to the home page of "Work Links".

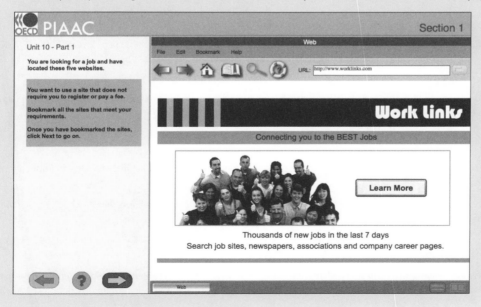

In order to discover whether access to the information on available jobs requires registration with the organisation or payment of a fee, the respondent must click the "Learn More" button which opens the following page. The respondent must then return to the search results page to continue evaluating the sites in terms of the specified criteria, using the back arrows without bookmarking the page (correct answer) or having bookmarked the page (incorrect answer).

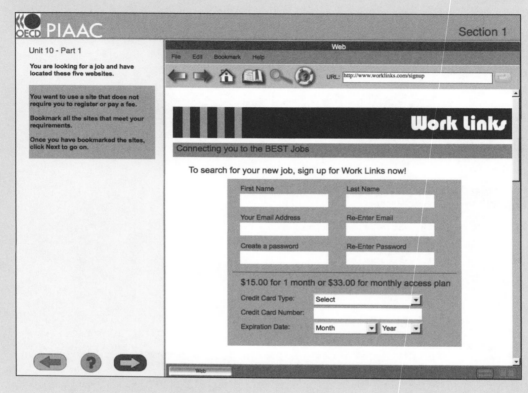

Notes

1. The concept of "key competencies" is discussed in greater detail in Chapter 7.

2. For the complete framework documents, see PIAAC Literacy Expert Group (2009), PIAAC Numeracy Expert Group (2009), PIAAC Expert Group in Problem Solving in Technology-Rich Environments (2009), and Sabatini and Bruce (2009).

3. The PISA 2009 assessment included a test of digital reading. This was implemented in 19 countries (OECD, 2011).

4. In particular, the survey was designed to be "adaptive" in that respondents were directed to different blocks of items based on their estimated proficiency. This is explained in more detail in Chapter 3.

References

European Commission (2007), *Key Competencies for Lifelong Learning: European Reference Framework*, Office for Official Publications of the European Communities, Luxembourg.

OECD (2012), *Literacy, Numeracy and Problem Solving in Technology-Rich Environments: Framework for the OECD Survey of Adult Skills*, OECD Publishing, Paris, http://dx.doi.org/10.1787/9789264128859-en.

OECD (2011), *PISA 2009 Results: Students on Line: Digital Technologies and Performance (Volume VI)*, OECD Publishing, Paris, http://dx.doi.org/10.1787/9789264112995-en.

PIAAC Expert Group in Problem Solving in Technology-Rich Environments (2009), "PIAAC Problem Solving in Technology-Rich Environments: A Conceptual Framework", *OECD Education Working Papers*, No. 36, OECD Publishing, Paris, http://dx.doi.org/10.1787/220262483674.

PIAAC Literacy Expert Group (2009), "PIAAC Literacy: A Conceptual Framework", *OECD Education Working Papers*, No. 34, OECD Publishing, Paris, http://dx.doi.org/10.1787/220348414075.

PIAAC Numeracy Expert Group (2009), "PIAAC Numeracy: A Conceptual Framework", *OECD Education Working Papers*, No. 35, OECD Publishing, Paris, http://dx.doi.org/10.1787/220337421165.

Sabatini, J. P. and **K. M. Bruce** (2009), "PIAAC Reading Component: A Conceptual Framework", *OECD Education Working Papers*, No. 33, OECD Publishing, Paris, http://dx.doi.org/10.1787/220367414132.

UNESCO (2005), *EFA Global Monitoring Report, 2006: Education for All, Literacy for Life*, UNESCO, Paris.

2

The background questionnaire of the Survey of Adult Skills (PIAAC)

This chapter describes the questionnaire that is part of the Survey of Adult Skills (PIAAC). The questionnaire collects information on the basic demographic characteristics of respondents; educational attainment and participation; labour force status and employment; social outcomes; the use of literacy, numeracy and ICT skills at work and in everyday life; and the use of a range of other skills at work.

The background questionnaire for the Survey of Adult Skills (PIAAC, 2010[1]) collects a comprehensive set of information designed to support the major analytical objectives of PIAAC, namely to:

- Determine the level and the distribution of proficiency in key information-processing skills for certain subgroups of the adult population.
- Better understand factors associated with the acquisition, development, maintenance and loss of proficiency over a lifetime.
- Better understand the relationship of proficiency in information-processing skills to economic and other social outcomes.

The development of the background questionnaire was overseen by the PIAAC Background Questionnaire Expert Group. The principles guiding the selection of the items included in the questionnaire can be found in the conceptual framework for the development of the background questionnaire (PIAAC, 2009). In addition to being relevant to the policy questions to which the Survey of Adult Skills was intended to respond, items were expected to measure concepts that had a strong theoretical underpinning, had been measured in other studies, and would be comparable across countries and groups within countries. In addition, efforts were made to maximise comparability with related surveys, such as the International Adult Literacy Survey (IALS) and the Adult Literacy and Life Skills Survey (ALL), as well as other cross-national surveys focusing on related topics, such as adult education and training, by using common items. Questions relevant to small subgroups were avoided. The target maximum duration of the background questionnaire (i.e. for an employed person who was participating in some formal education or training activity) was 45 minutes.

Participating countries/economies were requested to adapt questions to reflect national circumstances in domains such as educational attainment and participation, labour-force participation and employment, where institutional structures were nationally specific or where there were national protocols for collecting data. Countries/economies had the opportunity to add a small number of "national" questions to the national versions of the background questionnaire. These were expected to add no more than five minutes to the average duration of the questionnaire.

The background questionnaire collected information in five main areas:

- basic demographic characteristics and background of respondents
- educational attainment and participation
- labour-force status and employment
- social outcomes
- literacy and numeracy practices and the use of skills.

The information collected is described below, together with the rationale for including it in the questionnaire.

THE CHARACTERISTICS AND BACKGROUND OF RESPONDENTS

Understanding the distribution of proficiency across key subgroups of the adult population is one of the major objectives of the Survey of Adult Skills. To this end, in addition to information on the basic demographic variables of gender and age, the background questionnaire collects data regarding language background, immigration status, and social background (the educational level of the respondent's parents and the cultural capital of his/her family). Data on household and family structure is also collected, given the potential importance of these variables in explaining observed proficiency and as indicators of individual well being (Table 2.1).

Table 2.1 **Data collected concerning the characteristics and background of respondents**

Domain	Specific data items
Demographics	Age, gender, country of birth.
Household and family structure	Number of persons in household, living with spouse or partner, activity of spouse/partner, number and age of children.
Language background	First and second languages spoken when a child, language currently most often spoken at home.
Immigration status	Age at which respondent immigrated, country of birth of parents.
Social background	Highest level of education of parents, number of books in home at age 16.
Residential location	Location of residence.

EDUCATIONAL ATTAINMENT AND PARTICIPATION IN LEARNING ACTIVITIES

Participation in education and training activities, whether formal or non-formal,[2] is understood as both a factor explaining proficiency in the skills assessed and a possible outcome of having these skills. Literacy, numeracy and problem solving are, in part, developed through participation in education and training activities, such as schooling and other post-school education and training (e.g. vocational education and training, university, or workplace-based learning). At the same time, the level of proficiency in these skills is related to the probability of participating in learning activities following the completion of compulsory schooling.

The information collected on *formal* education and training experience covers the highest level of completed education, incomplete studies, and the age at which study was completed as well as participation in the 12 months preceding the interview. Information on participation in *non-formal* education and training during the 12 months prior to the interview is also collected. In line with most surveys of adult education and training, respondents are asked whether they face any barriers to participation in education and training (Table 2.2).

Table 2.2 **Information collected regarding educational experience and current participation in learning activities**

Domain	Specific data items
Educational experience	Highest qualification, in which country qualification gained, field of study of highest qualification, age completed highest qualification.
Current study	Undertaking formal study, level of course, field of study.
Incomplete study	Has started but not completed a course of formal study, level of course, age at which left course.
Formal studies in previous year	Undertaken formal studies in previous year, how many courses, level of last course, reason for undertaking study, employed while studying, study took place in or outside working hours, usefulness of course to work, type of employer support received.
Non-formal courses in previous 12 months	Undertaken different non-formal learning activities in previous 12 months (open or distance courses, organised on-the-job training, seminars or workshops, other courses), how many activities of each type.
Most recent non-formal activity	Type of activity, activity mainly job-related, main reason for participation, took place in or outside working hours, employer support provided.
Volume of participation in education and training in previous 12 months	Total time in education and training activities, proportion of time in job-related activities.
Barriers to undertaking education and training	Wanted to participate in learning activities in prior 12 months but did not, reasons preventing participation.
Learning style	Interest in learning, approach to new information.

LABOUR FORCE STATUS, WORK HISTORY AND JOB CHARACTERISTICS

The relationship of individuals' skills profiles to labour-force status, employment income and the characteristics of jobs is central to the Survey of Adult Skills. This information helps to establish the degree to which the assessed skills are related to labour force status and employment outcomes. In addition, an individual's activity status (e.g. work, unemployment, study) and, for those in employment, the characteristics of the workplace and the work the individual does, have a potentially significant impact on opportunities to maintain and develop the skills assessed.

The information collected concerning labour force status, work history, and job characteristics is presented in Table 2.3. Information on job characteristics is sought from both respondents in employment (their current job) and from those who are unemployed but who had been employed in the previous five years (their most recent job).

Table 2.3 Information collected regarding labour force status, work history and job characteristics

Domain	Specific data items
Current activity	Labour force status (ILO definition), main current activity.
Work history	Ever worked, had paid work in previous 12 months, age stopped working (if unemployed), total time in employment, number of employers in previous five years.
Current job	Industry, occupation, employee or self-employed, age started with current employer, establishment size, number of employees increasing or decreasing, part of larger organisation, (if self-employed) number of employees, management of supervisory responsibilities, number of subordinates, type of employment contract, usual working hours, extent of flexibility regarding job tasks, job satisfaction, gross wages or salary, (if self-employed) earnings from business.
Most recent job (if unemployed)	Industry, occupation, employee or self-employed, when left last employer, establishment size, (if self employed) number of employees, management of supervisory responsibilities, number of subordinates, type of employment contract, usual working hours, main reason for leaving last job.

SOCIAL PARTICIPATION AND HEALTH

Beyond the impact of proficiency in information-processing skills on labour market outcomes, such as employment, income and job satisfaction, there is growing interest in the relationship of proficiency to other "social" outcomes. The Survey of Adult Skills collects information on respondents' beliefs regarding society and the political process, participation in voluntary activities, and their self-reported health status.

Table 2.4 Information collected on social participation and health

Domain	Specific data items
Trust	Trust in others, perception of others' behaviour towards self.
Political efficacy	Influence on political process.
Volunteering	Frequency of voluntary work in previous 12 months.
Health status	Self-assessed health status.

THE USE OF SKILLS

The background questionnaire collects a range of information on the reading- and numeracy-related activities of respondents and ICT use at work and in everyday life, and on the generic skills required of individuals in their work. In addition, respondents are asked whether their skills and qualifications match their work requirements and whether they have autonomy over key aspects of their work.

These data are collected for a number of different but related reasons:

- Engagement in reading and numeracy practices and the use of ICTs are defined as important components of proficiency in literacy, numeracy and problem solving in technology-rich environments.
- The type and frequency of reading, numeracy-related activities and ICT use are important correlates of proficiency in the domains of literacy, numeracy and problem solving.
- There is considerable policy interest in obtaining information on a range of generic skills, in addition to literacy, numeracy and problem solving in technology-rich environments that are valued in the labour market.
- Policy makers are keen to learn more about the balance between the supply of and demand for skills and how to avoid skills mismatch.

Engagement as a component of proficiency

Engagement is an important element of literacy and numeracy in the Survey of Adult Skills. Literacy is defined as "understanding, evaluating, *using* and *engaging with* written texts". Similarly, engaging in numeracy-related practices is associated with proficient numerate behaviour (OECD, 2012a, p. 39). The mastery of foundation ICT skills is a prerequisite for proficiency in problem solving in technology-rich environments (OECD, 2012a, p. 51).

The role of literacy and numeracy practices and computer use in maintaining and developing skills

The Survey of Adult Skills seeks not only to describe the level and distribution of proficiency in the skills it measures, but also to provide information on factors associated with the acquisition, maintenance and development of these skills and their outcomes. It is clear that proficiency in cognitive skills, such as literacy and numeracy, are not fixed for life, and that life paths, interests and individuals' circumstances have an impact on the patterns of skills gain and loss. Engagement in literacy and numeracy practices and the use of ICTs in work and everyday life is one way adults enhance or maintain their skills. Empirical studies (see Desjardins, 2003) show that literacy proficiency is strongly related to literacy practices in work and other contexts. Proficiency and practice are mutually reinforcing, with practice positively affecting the level of proficiency and proficiency having a positive impact on practice.

Comparative information on a broader range of key skills

Cognitive skills, such as literacy, numeracy and problem solving, comprise just one cluster among the many different generic skills and attributes that are believed to be of value to the labour market. A range of non-cognitive skills, such as the capacity to work collaboratively or as a member of a team, communication skills, and entrepreneurship, is also of importance in the modern workplace, and there is considerable interest in comparative information on both the supply of and demand for such skills.

Since it was not feasible to directly and comparably measure these types of skills in the first cycle of the survey, respondents were asked about the different types of generic tasks that they perform in their jobs. The types of skills required for these tasks were then inferred from the respondents' answers.[3] This alternative to a direct assessment provides a more objective measure of skills than an approach that relies on respondents' self-reports on the types and level of skills they possess.

Demand for skills

The measures of adults' proficiency in literacy, numeracy and problem solving in technology-rich environments provide information on the *supply* of these skills. While skills supply is clearly of central importance for government policies, it is also important to understand how skills are being used in modern workplaces and how the demand for different types of skills is evolving. Optimising the use of skills is a central theme of the recent OECD Skills Strategy (OECD, 2012b) and in the World Bank's framework for skills development (STEP) (World Bank, 2010).

Closely linked to the demand for skills is the issue of the match/mismatch between the qualifications and skills that workers have and those that they use in their jobs. Researchers and policy makers have become increasingly interested in this topic over recent years (Cedefop, 2010; Desjardins and Rubenson, 2011; OECD, 2011; Skills Australia, 2010; UKCES, 2010).

The issue of match/mismatch has been investigated at a very broad level (e.g. at the level of qualifications) or by using respondents' perceptions (self-reports) of over- or under-qualification and over- and under-skilling. Combining information on the use of literacy, numeracy, problem solving and computing skills in the workplace with information on the proficiency of individuals provides a way of more objectively examining the incidence and consequences of match/mismatch between workers' skills and the demands of their jobs than has been possible previously, at least regarding the information-processing skills measured in the Survey of Adult Skills.

Skills use: Task clusters

Table 2.5 provides an overview of the clusters of tasks for which information is collected in the Survey of Adult Skills, the specific tasks included under each cluster, and the life domain (work or everyday life[4]) of the tasks. *Italics* indicate that information is sought both in work and in everyday life. Information is sought regarding the use of information-processing skills assessed in the survey (literacy, numeracy and problem solving), the requirements of jobs related to four clusters of "generic" job tasks (interaction, learning, organisation and planning, and physical/motor activity), and technological skills as demonstrated by using information technologies. For work tasks, information was collected from both currently employed respondents and from those who had had a job in the previous 12 months. Respondents in the latter group were asked to give information about their most recent job.

Table 2.5 **Information collected regarding tasks and activities in work and everyday life**

Task cluster	Life domain	Component activities
Cognitive skills		
Reading	Work Everyday life	*Read directions or instructions; letters, memos or e-mails; articles in newspapers, magazines or newsletters; articles in professional journals or scholarly publications; books; reference manuals or materials; bills, invoices, bank statements or financial statements; diagrams, maps, schematics.*
Writing	Work Everyday life	*Write letters, memos or e-mails; articles for newspapers, magazines or newsletters; reports; fill in forms.*
Numeracy	Work Everyday life	*Calculate prices, costs or budgets; use or calculate fractions, decimals or percentages; use a calculator (hand held or computer-based); prepare charts graphs or tables; use simple algebra or formulas;* use advanced maths or statistics.
Problem solving	Work	Solve simple problems; solve complex problems.
Technology		
ICT skills	Work Everyday life	*Use computer; e-mail; Internet for information; Internet to conduct monetary transactions; spreadsheets; word processing; write or prepare computer code; real-time discussions using Internet;* overall level of computer use in terms of complexity.
Interaction		
Co-operation	Work	Time spent collaborating; sharing of information with co-workers.
Influencing	Work	Selling products or services; making speeches or presentations; advising; persuading or influencing others; negotiating; instructing, training or teaching others.
Learning		
Learning	Work	Learning from others; learning by doing; keeping up to date with new products or services.
Organisation		
Organisation and planning	Work	Planning own activities; planning activities of others; organising own time.
Physical		
Physical requirements	Work	Working physically for long periods; use of fine motor skills.

Note: Italics indicate that information is sought about the use of the skills concerned in both work and everyday life.

Literacy or numeracy practices, both in work and in everyday life, and work tasks can be described by their:

- incidence (whether or not a given task/activity is performed)
- variety (the diversity of tasks or activities that are performed or undertaken)
- frequency (the frequency with which a given task or activity is performed or undertaken)
- complexity/difficulty (the level of cognitive demand or competency required to perform the task/activity successfully)
- criticality (the importance of the task or activity to the performance of the job).

In each broad task cluster a number of specific tasks or activities are identified. For example, respondents are questioned about the extent to which they read different types of materials (e.g. instructions, diagrams, newspaper articles, books) and are also asked to cite the frequency with which they engage in each of these activities on a scale ranging from "never" to "every day". A similar approach is adopted for other generic work tasks. While an attempt is made to cover the range of practices in which individuals may engage in a given domain, differentiating practices according to complexity is not easy.

The complexity of reading tasks depends on many factors that are unrelated to the text type (e.g. a book or a scholarly article). Criteria such as the length of the text are also likely to be only loosely related to difficulty and complexity. The "criticality" of a task or its relative priority in meeting the performance expectations in a given job[5] is not examined.

Twelve skill use indices have been derived covering both cognitive and generic skills. These are detailed in Table 2.6. The methodology for their derivation is outlined in Box 2.1.

Table 2.6 **Skills use indicators**

Indicator	Group of tasks
Information Processing skills	
Reading	Reading documents (directions, instructions, letters, memos, e-mails, articles, books, manuals, bills, invoices, diagrams, maps).
Writing	Writing documents (letters, memos, e-mails, articles, reports, forms).
Numeracy	Calculating prices, costs or budgets; use of fractions, decimals or percentages; use of calculators; preparing graphs or tables; algebra or formulas; use of advanced maths or statistics (calculus, trigonometry, regressions).
ICT skills	Using e-mail, Internet, spreadsheets, word processors, programming languages; conducting transactions online; participating in online discussions (conferences, chats).
Problem solving	Facing hard problems (at least 30 minutes of thinking to find a solution).
Other generic skills	
Task discretion	Choosing or changing sequence of job tasks, the speed of work, working hours; choosing how to do the job.
Learning at work	Learning new things from supervisors or co-workers; learning-by-doing; keeping up to date with new products or services.
Influencing skills	Instructing, teaching or training people; making speeches or presentations; selling products or services; advising people; planning others' activities; persuading or influencing others; negotiating.
Co-operative skills	Co-operating or collaborating with co-workers.
Self-organising skills	Organising time.
Physical skills (gross)	Working physically for a long period.
Dexterity	Using skill or accuracy with hands or fingers.

Box 2.1 **Using Item Response Theory to derive skills use indicators in the Survey of Adults Skills (PIAAC)**

Item Response Theory (IRT) is the most appropriate methodology to combine multiple items (i.e. multiple choice questions) from a questionnaire or an assessment exercise to derive measures of an underlying unobservable psychometric trait, such as the ability of the individuals, or how frequently individuals use certain types of skills at work.

The background questionnaire of the Survey of Adult Skills (PIAAC) includes two detailed sections with a set of items attempting to capture information to estimate latent scales related to generic and foundation skills used at work. The main characteristic of these items is the ordering behind the structure of the possible answers, whereby consecutive alternatives always indicate a higher frequency of performing a certain task (ranging from 0, corresponding to never performing the corresponding task, to 4, corresponding to performing the task every day).

...

The generalised partial credit model (GPCM) is an IRT model developed for situations where the item responses are contained in two or more ordered categories. Items associated to a given latent trait are grouped together and the unobserved trait is estimated. The main ingredients for the estimation are (a) the unidimensionality of the latent construct or scale and (b) the parameterisation of the model allowing mapping each level on the latent scale to the probability of choosing a specific alternative among the item possible choices over the immediate precedent. The resulting scale is a continuous one-dimensional construct that explains the covariance among the item responses: people with a higher level on the derived scale have a higher probability of frequently performing the task detailed in a given item.

Individuals who report "never" performing any of the tasks included in each IRT scales are excluded from these scales. This is done for two reasons. First, a zero-inflated-count issue arises for some of these items. For instance, a large group of individuals report "never" performing any of the tasks underlying the reading, numeracy, and writing at work scales, these groups are so large that they cannot be reasonably included in the population of those who have a degree of skill use ranging from high to low. Second, the items used to calculate the scales related to ICT skills use at work and at home are only asked to people who report having used a computer before, thus few individuals report "never" using their ICT skills at work. As a result, including individuals reporting "never" performing tasks in other scales would have created a difference with the ICT scale.

The IRT methodology produces reliable skills measures only with a sufficient number of items and for some domains too few were available in the Survey of Adult Skills. As a consequence, 5 of the 12 skills use indicators were derived directly from one individual item of the questionnaire, namely problem solving, co-operative skills, self-organising skills, physical skills and dexterity. These direct measures take five possible values, ranging from 0, corresponding to never performing the corresponding task, to 4, corresponding to performing the task every day. All the other IRT-derived indices are continuous variables, which should be interpreted as representing the level of use of the underlying skill and, for easier comparisons, have all been standardised to have mean equal to 2 and standard deviation equal to 1 across the pooled sample of respondents in all countries/economies (appropriately weighted). This results in indices for which at least 90% of the observations lay between 0 and 4, whereby values approaching 0 suggest a low frequency of use and values approaching 4 suggest a high frequency.

While the careful co-ordination of the survey design guarantees that results can be meaningfully compared across countries/economies, the standardisation of the IRT-derived skills use indicators means that comparisons across skill domains should be taken as suggestive. Indeed, besides the metric, such comparisons are problematic for reasons that go beyond the choice of the indicators, as skills are often conceptually different notions and the forms of their interplay are difficult to ascertain. For example, when evaluating the productive returns to the use of skills one may wonder whether a moderate use of ICT is more or less productive than an intensive use of reading or writing.

In addition to questions relating to the tasks and activities that they perform in their work, respondents are asked some broad questions relating to the match of their skills, qualifications and experience to those needed to get and/or do their jobs. These cover both general skills and qualifications as well as computing skills (Table 2.7).

Table 2.7 **Information collected on aspects of qualifications and skills match/mismatch**

	Components
Self-assessment of match of skills and job requirements	Has skills to cope with more demanding duties; requires more training to cope with duties; level of computer use needed to perform job; possesses sufficient computer skills to do job well; lack of computer skills has affected chances of promotion or pay rise.
Match of qualifications to job requirements	Educational qualification needed to get current job; this qualification needed to do the job; related work experience needed to get the job.

In Chapter 4 of *OECD Skills Outlook* (OECD, 2013), a novel indicator of skills mismatch is derived combining information on self-reported skills match/mismatch, skills use and proficiency in literacy, numeracy and problem solving. The derivation of this indicator is described in Box 2.2.

Box 2.2 **Deriving the survey's measures of skills mismatch in literacy, numeracy or problem solving**

The Survey of Adult Skills (PIAAC) allows for producing a more robust measure of skills mismatch than the two commonly used in the literature, namely self-reported skills mismatch and measures derived by the direct comparison of skill proficiency with skills use at work. Indeed, both these methodologies are unsatisfactory and their limitations have been highlighted in the literature. When asked directly, workers in most countries/economies tend to be highly over-confident: too many of them report being qualified to perform more demanding jobs, thus undermining the validity of skills mismatch measures based on self-reported information. On the other hand, the comparison of skills proficiency and skills use rests on the assumption that the two can be measured on the same scale, an assumption that is very difficult to defend for concepts that are so clearly distinct theoretically and that cannot be represented along the same metrics (Krahn and Lowe, 1998). Additionally, the measures of skills proficiency and skills use are based on structurally different pieces of information: indicators of skills use normally exploit survey questions about the frequency (and/or the importance) with which specific tasks are carried out in the respondents' work activities, whereas skills proficiency is usually measured through foundation tests.

Using the Survey of Adult Skills, it is possible to combine three pieces of information, namely self-reported skills mismatch, skills use and skills proficiency, into a novel indicator of skills mismatch derived as follows:

- **Step 1.** Identify workers who self-report being well-matched as those workers who neither feel they have the skills to perform a more demanding job nor feel the need of further training in order to be able to perform their current jobs satisfactorily.

- **Step 2.** For each skill dimension (literacy, numeracy and problem solving), define the minimum and maximum skill level required in an occupation as the minimum and the maximum proficiency of self-reported well-matched workers (defined as in Step 1) by country and within each 1-digit International Standard Classification of Occupations (ISCO) code. To limit the potential impact of outliers on these measurements, it is useful to use the 5th and the 95th percentile instead of the actual minimum and maximum. Because of sample size, ISCO group 0 (armed forces) and ISCO group 6 (skilled agricultural workers) were dropped and ISCO group 1 was merged to ISCO group 2 for the purpose of calculating skill requirements.

- **Step 3.** For each skills dimension (literacy, numeracy and problem solving), classify workers as under-skilled if their proficiency is lower than the minimum requirement in their occupation and country and as over-skilled if their proficiency is higher than the maximum requirement in their occupation and country. All other workers are classified as well-matched.

The above procedure allows for calculating the shares of workers who are under-skilled, well-matched and over-skilled in each occupation and for each skill. In a further step, the skills use of workers who are over- and under-skilled is compared with that of equally-proficient workers – i.e. workers with similar proficiency scores – who are well-matched.

Notes

1. The international "master" version of the questionnaire used in the Survey of Adult Skills (PIAAC) can be accessed at: www.oecd.org/dataoecd/1/41/48442549.pdf.

2. "Formal" education and training comprises education that is institutionalised, intentional and planned through public organisations and recognised private bodies. "Non-formal" education is institutionalised, intentional and planned by an education provider. Non-formal education mostly leads to qualifications that are not recognised as formal qualifications by the relevant national educational authorities or to no qualifications at all (see UNESCO, 2011).

3. This draws on the approach pioneered in the UK Skills Survey – the so-called Jobs Requirements Approach or JRA (see Felstead et. al, 2007).

4. "Everyday life" covers all non-work related activities, including study.

5. For an orthopaedic surgeon, tasks related to surgical interventions will be more critical for the definition of his or her job than tasks relating to communication, even if writing reports and sharing information with colleagues are frequent occurrences.

References

Cedefop (2010), *The Skill Matching Challenge: Analysing Skill Mismatch and Policy Implications*, Publications Office of the European Union, Luxembourg.

Desjardins, R. (2003), "Determinants of Literacy Proficiency: A Lifelong-lifewide Learning Perspective", *International Journal of Educational Research*, Vol. 39, pp. 205-245.

Desjardins, R. and **K. Rubenson** (2011), "An Analysis of Skill Mismatch Using Direct Measures of Skills", *OECD Education Working Papers*, No. 63, OECD Publishing, Paris, http://dx.doi.org/10.1787/5kg3nh9h52g5-en.

Felstead, A., D. Gallie, F. Green and **Y. Zhou** (2007), *Skills at Work, 1986 to 2006*, ESRC Centre on Skills, Knowledge and Organisational Performance, Oxford and Cardiff.

Krahn, H. and **G. Lowe** (1998), "Literacy Utilization in Canadian Workplaces", Statistics Canada, Catalogue No. 89-552-MIE, No. 4.

OECD (2013), *OECD Skills Outlook: First Results from the Survey of Adult Skills*, OECD Publishing, Paris, http://dx.doi.org/10.1787/9789264204256-en.

OECD (2012a), *Literacy, Numeracy and Problem Solving in Technology-Rich Environments: Framework for the OECD Survey of Adult Skills*, OECD Publishing, Paris, http://dx.doi.org/10.1787/9789264128859-en.

OECD (2012b), *Better Skills, Better Jobs, Better Lives: A Strategic Approach to Skills Policies*, OECD Publishing, Paris, http://dx.doi.org/10.1787/9789264177338-en.

OECD (2011), *OECD Employment Outlook 2011*, OECD Publishing, Paris, http://dx.doi.org/10.1787/empl_outlook-2011-en.

PIAAC (2010), "PIAAC Background Questionnaire", OECD Programme for the International Assessment of Adult Competencies, www.oecd.org/dataoecd/1/41/48442549.pdf.

PIAAC (2009), "PIAAC Background Questionnaire JRA V5.0: Conceptual Framework", OECD Programme for the International Assessment of Adult Competencies, www.oecd.org/edu/48865373.pdf.

Skills Australia (2010), *Australian Workforce Futures: A National Workforce Development Strategy*, Skills Australia.

UK Commission for Employment and Skills (UKCES) (2010), *Skills for Jobs: Today and Tomorrow – The National Strategic Skills Audit for England 2010 – Volume 2: The Evidence Report*, UK Commission for Employment and Skills.

UNESCO (2011), *Revision of the International Standard Classification of Education (ISCED)*, Paper 36 C/19, 34th session of the General Conference, 2011, UNESCO, www.uis.unesco.org/Education/Documents/UNESCO_GC_36C-19_ISCED_EN.pdf.

World Bank (2010), *Stepping Up Skills for More Jobs and Higher Productivity*, the World Bank Group, Washington, DC.

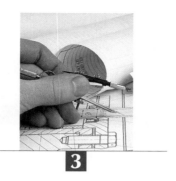

3

The methodology of the Survey of Adult Skills (PIAAC) and the quality of data

This chapter focuses on how the Survey of Adult Skills (PIAAC) was designed, managed and conducted. It discusses the target population, exclusions from the survey, sample size, response rates, and how the survey was scored.

A note regarding Israel

The statistical data for Israel are supplied by and under the responsibility of the relevant Israeli authorities. The use of such data by the OECD is without prejudice to the status of the Golan Heights, East Jerusalem and Israeli settlements in the West Bank under the terms of international law.

To date the Survey of Adult Skills has involved two rounds of data collection: the first involving 24 countries/economies and the second nine. The first round of the study extended from January 2008 to October 2013. The second extended from January 2012 until June 2016. Table 3.1 presents the dates of key phases of the two rounds as well as listing the countries/economies participating in each.

Table 3.1 **List of participating countries and economies and dates of key phases**

	Round 1	Round 2
Project start	January 2008	2011
Field test	April to June 2010	April to June 2013
Main study data collection	August 2011 to November 2012	April 2014 to March 2015
Report and data release	13 October 2013	28 June 2016
Participating countries and economies	Australia	Chile
	Austria	Greece
	Canada	Israel
	Cyprus[1]	Jakarta (Indonesia)
	Czech Republic	Lithuania
	Denmark	New Zealand
	England (United Kingdom)	Singapore
	Estonia	Slovenia
	Flanders (Belgium)	Turkey
	Finland	
	France	
	Germany	
	Ireland	
	Italy	
	Japan	
	Korea	
	Netherlands	
	Northern Ireland (United Kingdom)	
	Norway	
	Poland	
	Russian Federation[2]	
	Slovak Republic	
	Spain	
	Sweden	
	United States	

1. *Note by Turkey:* The information in this document with reference to "Cyprus" relates to the southern part of the Island. There is no single authority representing both Turkish and Greek Cypriot people on the Island. Turkey recognises the Turkish Republic of Northern Cyprus (TRNC). Until a lasting and equitable solution is found within the context of the United Nations, Turkey shall preserve its position concerning the "Cyprus issue".

Note by all the European Union Member States of the OECD and the European Union: The Republic of Cyprus is recognised by all members of the United Nations with the exception of Turkey. The information in this document relates to the area under the effective control of the Government of the Republic of Cyprus.

2. See note at the end of this chapter.

Countries and economies are ranked in alphabetical order.

Both rounds of PIAAC were guided by the same set of technical standards and guidelines (PIAAC, 2014) developed to ensure that the survey yielded high-quality and internationally comparable data. The *PIAAC Technical Standards and Guidelines* articulates the standards to which participating countries/economies were expected to adhere in implementing the assessment, describes the steps that should be followed in order to meet the standards, and offers recommendations for actions relating to the standards that were not mandatory but that could help to produce high quality data. Standards were established for 16 discrete aspects of the design and implementation of the survey (Table 3.2).

Table 3.2 **Areas of activity covered by the PIAAC Standards and Guidelines**

Survey instruments	Data collection staff training
Translation and adaptation	Data collection
Information technology	Data capture
Field management	Data file creation
Quality assurance and quality control	Confidentiality and data security
Ethics	Weighting
Survey planning	Estimation
Sample design (including survey response and non-response bias)	Documentation

The *PIAAC Technical Standards and Guidelines* is one element of a comprehensive process of quality assurance and control that was put in place to reduce potential sources of error and maximise the quality of the data produced by the Survey of Adult Skills. Participating countries/economies received assistance in meeting the standards in a variety of ways. Where relevant, manuals, training materials, testing plans and toolkits were produced. Training was provided to countries at appropriate stages of the project. In certain areas, such as sampling, translation and adaptation, and the operation of the computer-delivery platform, passage through the various stages of implementation was subject to a review of the steps completed, and sign-off was often required as a condition of moving to a subsequent stage. Regular consultations were held with countries at project meetings and through bilateral contact. Compliance with the technical standards was monitored throughout the development and implementation phases through direct contact, evidence that required activities were completed, and the ongoing collection of data from countries concerning key aspects of implementation.

The quality of each participating country's data was reviewed prior to publication. The review was based on the analysis of the psychometric characteristics of the data and evidence of compliance with the technical standards. An assessment of the quality of each country's data was prepared and recommendations were made regarding release and, if necessary, restrictions and/or qualifications that should apply to the release and publication. The approach to the review of data was validated by the project's Technical Advisory team; the project's steering body, the PIAAC Board of Participating Countries (BPC), made the final decision on release.

Box 3.1 **How the Survey of Adult Skills (PIAAC) was managed**

The development and implementation of the Survey of Adult Skills (PIAAC) was overseen by the PIAAC Board of Participating Countries (BPC). The Board consisted of representatives from each of the countries participating in the survey, with the exception of Cyprus[1] and the Russian Federation. The Board was responsible for making major decisions regarding budgets, the development and implementation of the survey, reporting of results, and for monitoring the progress of the project. The Board was supported in its work by the OECD Secretariat, which was responsible for providing advice to the Board and managing the project on behalf of the Board.

An international Consortium was contracted by the OECD to undertake a range of tasks relating to the design and development of the assessment, implementation and analysis. The Consortium was responsible for developing questionnaires, instruments, and the computer-delivery platform, supporting survey operations, quality control, and scaling, preparing the database, and providing support for analysis.

Participating countries/economies were responsible for the national implementation of the assessment. This covered sampling, adaptation and translation of assessment materials, data collection and database production. In each country, national project teams were led by national project managers.

This chapter focuses on aspects of the design and the methodology of the Survey of Adult Skills that are essential for interpreting the results of the data-quality review. To this end, it describes:

- the design of the assessment and administration of the survey
- sampling
- translation and adaptation of instruments
- survey administration
- survey response
- scoring
- the outcomes of the adjudication of data quality.

ASSESSMENT DESIGN

The Survey of Adult Skills involved the direct assessment of literacy, numeracy and problem solving in technology-rich environments. While conceived primarily as a computer-based assessment (CBA), the option of taking the literacy and numeracy components of the assessment in paper-based format (PBA) had to be provided for those adults who had insufficient experience with computers to take the assessment in CBA mode. This necessitated a relatively complex design, which is presented graphically in Figure 3.1.

In Jakarta (Indonesia), the assessment was delivered in paper-based format only due to the low rate of familiarity with computers among the target population. This was a version of the paper-based assessment used in other countries that included additional items.

Pathways through the cognitive assessments in the Survey of Adult Skills (PIAAC): Computer-based assessment

As can be seen, there are several pathways through the computer-based assessment. Respondents with no experience in using computers, as indicated by their response to the relevant questions in the background questionnaire, were directed to the paper-based version of the assessment. Respondents with some experience of computer use were directed to the computer-based assessment where they took a short test of their ability to use the basic features of the test application (use of a mouse, typing, use of highlighting, and drag and drop functionality) – the CBA core Stage 1. Those who "failed" this component were directed to the paper pathway.

Figure 3.1 ■ **Pathways through the cognitive assessments in the Survey of Adult Skills (PIAAC): Computer-based assessment**

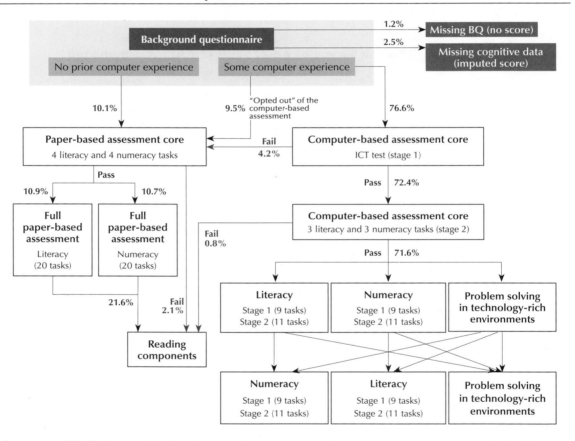

Note: The figures presented in this diagram are based on the average of OECD countries and economies participating in the Survey of Adult Skills (PIAAC).

Respondents taking the computer path then took a short test (the CBA core Stage 2) composed of three literacy and three numeracy items of low difficulty to determine whether or not they should continue with the full assessment. Those who "failed" this module were directed to the reading components assessment. Respondents who passed this module continued on to take the full test and were randomly assigned to a first module of literacy, numeracy or problem-solving items. Following completion of the first module, respondents who had completed a literacy module were randomly assigned to a numeracy or problem-solving module, respondents who had completed a numeracy module were randomly assigned to a literacy or problem-solving module, and respondents who had completed a problem-solving module were randomly assigned to a literacy, a numeracy or a second problem-solving module.

The assessment design assumed that the respondents taking the PBA path would be either those who had no prior experience with computers (as assessed on the basis of responses to the relevant questions in the background questionnaire) or those who failed the ICT core. It was, however, possible for respondents with some computer experience to take the PBA pathway if they insisted. Respondents with some computer experience who opted to take the paper-based pathway without attempting the CBA core represented 9.5% of all respondents in Rounds 1 and 2.

Respondents taking the paper path first took a "core" test of four simple literacy and four simple numeracy items. Those who passed this test were randomly assigned to a module of either 20 literacy tasks or 20 numeracy tasks. Once the module was completed, respondents were given the reading-components test. Respondents who failed the initial "core" test proceeded directly to the reading-components test.

Some 76.6% of respondents attempted the CBA core Stage 1. In total, 72.4 % of respondents took the CBA core Stage 2 and 71.6% of the sample went on to the CBA literacy, numeracy or problem solving assessment with 0.8% being directed to the reading components assessment.

Some 23.8% of respondents took the PBA assessment core and 21.6% went on to complete the paper-based literacy and numeracy assessment modules and the reading components assessment. A total of 2.9% of respondents completed the reading components assessment only. There was a small proportion of respondents who did not complete the cognitive assessment.

The Survey of Adult Skills was designed to provide accurate estimates of proficiency in the three domains across the adult population and its major subgroups, rather than at the level of individuals. Each respondent was given a subset of the test items used in the assessment. No individual took modules from all the domains assessed.

Table 3.3 **Participation in the cognitive-assessment modules**

OECD countries and economies	Literacy and numeracy	Problem solving in technology-rich environments	Reading components
Australia	Yes	Yes	Yes
Austria	Yes	Yes	Yes
Canada	Yes	Yes	Yes
Chile	Yes	Yes	Yes
Czech Republic	Yes	Yes	Yes
Denmark	Yes	Yes	Yes
England (UK)	Yes	Yes	Yes
Estonia	Yes	Yes	Yes
Finland	Yes	Yes	No
Flanders (Belgium)	Yes	Yes	Yes
France	Yes	No	No
Germany	Yes	Yes	Yes
Greece	Yes	Yes	Yes
Ireland	Yes	Yes	Yes
Israel	Yes	Yes	Yes
Italy	Yes	No	Yes
Japan	Yes	Yes	No
Korea	Yes	Yes	Yes
Netherlands	Yes	Yes	Yes
New Zealand	Yes	Yes	Yes
Northern Ireland (UK)	Yes	Yes	Yes
Norway	Yes	Yes	Yes
Poland	Yes	Yes	Yes
Slovak Republic	Yes	Yes	Yes
Slovenia	Yes	Yes	Yes
Spain	Yes	No	Yes
Sweden	Yes	Yes	Yes
Turkey	Yes	Yes	Yes
United States	Yes	Yes	Yes
Partners			
Cyprus[1]	Yes	No	Yes
Jakarta (Indonesia)	Yes	No	Yes
Lithuania	Yes	Yes	Yes
Russian Federation[2]	Yes	Yes	No
Singapore	Yes	Yes	Yes

1. See note 1 under Table 3.1.
2. See note at the end of this chapter.
Countries and economies are ranked in alphabetical order.

As can be seen from Figure 3.1, respondents following the CBA path took two assessment modules in either one or two of the three assessment domains.[2] Respondents following the PBA path took either a literacy or a numeracy module.

In the CBA mode, the literacy and numeracy assessments had an adaptive design. Respondents were directed to different blocks of items on the basis of their estimated ability. Individuals who were estimated to have greater proficiency were more likely to be directed to groups of more difficult items than those who were estimated to be less proficient. Each of the literacy and numeracy modules was composed of two stages containing testlets (groups of items) of varying difficulty. Stage 1 contained three testlets and Stage 2, four. Respondents' chances of being assigned to testlets of a certain difficulty depended on their level of educational attainment, whether their native language was the same as the test language, their score on the literacy/numeracy core and, if relevant, their score on a Stage 1 testlet.[3]

All participating countries/economies were required to administer the literacy and numeracy components of the assessments. Administration of the problem solving in technology-rich environments and the reading-components assessments was optional. All but four countries administered the problem-solving assessment, and all but three administered the reading components assessment. Table 3.3 provides details of participation in each of the cognitive assessments.

SAMPLING

To maximise the comparability of results, countries/economies participating in the Survey of Adult Skills were expected to meet stringent standards relating to the target population, sample design, sample selection response rates, and non-response bias analysis.

Table 3.4 **Sampling frames for countries/economies with registry samples**

OECD countries and economies	Sampling frame		
	Stage 1	Stage 2	Stage 3
Austria	Population registry, 2011		
Flanders (Belgium)	Population registry, 2011		
Denmark	Population registry, 2011		
Estonia	Population registry, 2011		
Finland	Statistics Finland's population database (based on the Central Population Register), 2011		
Germany	German Census Bureau frame of communities, 2011	Local population registries, 2011	
Italy	National Statistical Institute of Italy, 2011	Household registries held by municipalities, 2011	Population registries, 2011; combined with field enumeration
Japan	Resident registry, 2011	Resident registry, 2011	
Netherlands	Population registry, 2011		
Norway	Population registry, 2011		
Poland	Population registry, 2011	Population registry, 2011	
Slovak Republic	Population registry, 2011	Population registry, 2011	
Spain	Population registry, 2011	Population registry, 2011	
Sweden	Population registry, 2011		
Israel (small localities)	List of localities from Israeli Ministry of the Interior adjusted to the target population of the survey, 2013	Population registry, 2013	
Israel (big localities)	Population registry, 2013		
Singapore	Population registry, 2014		
Slovenia	Population registry, 2014		

Note: The grey shading indicates that there is no such stage in the country's/economy's sample design.

Table 3.5 **Sampling frames for countries using master samples**

Country	Sampling frame			
	Stage 1	Stage 2	Stage 3	Stage 4
Australia	Bureau of Statistics population survey master sample, 2006	Bureau of Statistics population survey master sample, 2006	Bureau of Statistics population survey master sample, 2006	Field enumeration
France	Master sample from census data file, 2010	Individual taxation file, 2010		

Note: The grey shading indicates that there is no such stage in the country's sample design.
No country/economy in Round 2 used a master sample as a sampling frame.

Table 3.6 **Sampling frames for countries/economies using area samples**

OECD countries and economies	Sampling frame			
	Stage 1	Stage 2	Stage 3	Stage 4
Canada	Short-form census returns, 2011	Short-form census returns, 2011	Field enumeration	
Cyprus[1]	CYSTAT – Census of Population (2001) updated with Electricity Authority of Cyprus (EAC) registry (2010)	CYSTAT – Census of Population (2001) updated with Electricity Authority of Cyprus (EAC) registry (2010)		
Czech Republic	Territorial Identification Register of Buildings and Addresses (UIR-ADR), 2010	Territorial Identification Register of Buildings and Addresses (UIR-ADR), 2010	Field enumeration	Field enumeration
England (UK)	Royal Mail list of UK Postal Sectors, 2011	Royal Mail PAF residential file, 2011	Field enumeration	Field enumeration
Ireland	Small Area classifications, 2009	Geodirectory (national address database), 2011	Field enumeration	
Korea	2010 Census	2010 Census	Field enumeration	
Northern Ireland (UK)	NI(POINTER) database, 2011	Field enumeration	Field enumeration	
United States	Census Bureau Population Estimates, 2008	2000 Census Bureau Summary File 1 (SF1), 2000; updated with data from the United States Postal Service 2010	Field enumeration	Field enumeration
Chile	2002 Census of Population and Housing, updated with 2012 population growth models	List of blocks provided by the National Statistics Institute, 2002 (rural) or 2008 (urban)	Field enumeration	Field enumeration
Greece	2011 Census	Field enumeration	Field enumeration	
Jakarta (Indonesia)	2010 Census	Field enumeration	Field enumeration	
Lithuania	Address database from the Registry of Addresses of Lithuania, 2013/2014	Address database from the Registry of Addresses of Lithuania, 2013/2014	Field enumeration	
New Zealand	Statistics New Zealand's Household Survey Frame, 2013	2013 Census Meshblocks	Field enumeration	Field enumeration
Turkey	List of Provinces, 2013	List of household addresses provided by the Turkish Statistical Institute, 2012	Field enumeration	

Note: The grey shading indicates that there is no such stage in the country's/economy's sample design.
1. See note 1 under Table 3.1.
No country/economy in Round 2 used a master sample as a sampling frame.

The target population and sampling frame

The target population for the survey consisted of the non-institutionalised population, aged 16-65 years, residing in the country at the time of data collection, irrespective of nationality, citizenship or language status. The normal territorial unit covered by the survey was that of the country as a whole. However, in three countries the sample frame covered subunits of the national territory. In Round 1, only the Flemish region (Flanders) participated in the survey in Belgium and in the United Kingdom, only the autonomous administrative regions of England and Northern Ireland participated. In Round 2, in Indonesia, only the Jakarta municipal area participated in the survey. Following the tsunami of March 2011, Japan had to revise its sample design to exclude affected regions. In the case of the Russian Federation, the results relate to the territory of the Russian Federation *excluding* the Moscow municipal area. Moscow was excluded after the data collection had been completed due to problems with a data collection in this area.

The sampling frame used by participating countries/economies at each stage of sample selection was required to be up-to-date and include only one record for each member of the target population. Multi-stage sample designs require a sampling frame for each stage of selection.

The sampling frames used by participating countries/economies were of three broad types: population registers (administrative lists of residents maintained at either national or regional level); master samples (lists of dwelling units or primary sampling units maintained at national level for official surveys); or area frames (a frame of geographic clusters formed by combining adjacent geographic areas, respecting their population sizes and taking into consideration travel distances for interviewers). The frames used by countries/economies at different stages of the sample selection are described in Tables 3.4 to 3.6.

Table 3.7 **Exclusions from target population**

OECD countries and economies	Exclusions (frame)	Exclusions (frame) % of target population	Exclusions (data collection) % of target population
Australia	Persons living in very remote areas, discrete indigenous communities (DIC), or non-institutional special dwellings; non-Australian diplomats, their staff and household members of such; members (and their dependents) of non-Australian defence forces	3.3	N/A
Austria	Illegal immigrants	0.6	0.8
Canada	Residents of smallest communities in the northern territories; residents of remote and very low population density areas in provinces; and persons living in non-institutional collective dwellings, other than students in residences	1.8	N/A
Chile	The following areas of Chile: Ollague, Isla de Pascua, Juan Fernández, Cochamó, Futaleufú, Hualaihué, Palena, Guaitecas, O'Higgins Tortel, Cabo de Hornos and Antártica. Also, given the practice of only listing eligible dwelling units (DUs), there is some unknown level of noncoverage due to ineligible DUs becoming eligible by the time of data collection. However, given the vacancy and moving rates in Chile, this is expected to be minor	0.1+	N/A
Czech Republic	Professional armed forces; municipalities with < 200 habitants	1.8	N/A
Denmark	Illegal immigrants	<0.1	5.0
England (UK)	Individuals living in private residences that are not listed on the "residential" version of the Postal Address File (PAF)	2.0	N/A
Estonia	Persons without a detailed address; illegal immigrants (no estimate provided)	2.8	0.6
Finland	Illegal immigrants; asylum-seekers	0.2	0.5
Flanders (Belgium)	Illegal immigrants	1.0	4.0
France	Young adults who have never claimed any income and are not attached to their parents households; some illegal immigrants	≤2.6	1.4
Germany	Illegal immigrants; other people who are not in the register (e.g. recently moved)	0.5	2.0
Greece	Persons residing in non-institutional group quarters	1.4	N/A
Ireland	Some mobile dwellings, such as the caravans of Irish travellers	0.4	N/A
Israel	Non-citizens	2.5	2.5
Italy	Adults in non-institutional group quarters; illegal immigrants (no estimate provided)	0.8	1.9
Japan	Non-nationals; illegal immigrants	2.2	2.8
Korea	Residents of small islands	2.4	N/A
Netherlands	Illegal immigrants	0.9	1.8
New Zealand	Persons living in off-shore islands; persons living in primary sample units (PSUs) with less than 9 occupied dwellings; persons in non-private dwellings and in private temporary dwellings	2.3	N/A
Northern Ireland (UK)	Individuals not listed on the NI(POINTER) database	2.0	N/A
Norway	Illegal immigrants	0.4	0.4
Poland	Foreigners staying in Poland less than three months; non-registered immigrants	0.8	4.2
Slovak Republic	Illegal immigrants	0.1	4.9
Slovenia	1.7% of small PSUs; a third of people aged 16 and 65;[3] people in workers quarters; foreigners who have been in the country less than one year but plan to stay; illegal immigrants	1.7	3.3
Spain	None	0.0	5.0
Sweden	Illegal immigrants	<1.0	0.0
Turkey	People who move into vacant dwelling units after the dwelling lists were constructed and before data collection ends	2.0	N/A
United States	Some Hispanics and black males (and other hard-to-reach groups) as in other US household surveys	<1.0	0.0
Partners			
Cyprus[1]	Persons living in houses built after December 2010	<2.0	N/A
Jakarta (Indonesia)	Population in RT/RWs not listed in the 2010 census	Unknown	N/A
Lithuania	Undocumented immigrants; Neringa (hard-to-reach region separated from rest of Lithuania by sea); villages with less than 20 addresses (these villages are almost vacant in most cases). Also, when listing DUs to create the frame, the field staff identified and excluded the streets which were found to have no DUs.	2.7	N/A
Russian Federation[2]	Chechnya region	1.5	N/A
Singapore	None[4]	0.0	0.6

1. See note 1 under Table 3.1.

2. See note at the end of this chapter.

3. PIAAC Guideline 4.1.1C requires countries/economies to use age at the mid-point of data collection to define the sampling frame of age eligible persons. However, Slovenia included only persons who are of an eligible age throughout the whole 8-month data collection period. As a result, a third of people aged 16 and aged 65 were excluded from the frame.

4. Singapore modified the definition of the target population to be all non-institutionalised Singapore citizens and Singapore permanent residents between the ages of 16 and 65 (inclusive) residing in Singapore at the time of data collection. Contract/temporary foreign workers are not considered part of their target population. There are 1.3 million people (approximately 25% of the total population) who are working, studying or living in Singapore but not granted permanent residence, and although they are part of the work force, live in housing, purchase goods and travel freely within the country, they are excluded from the target population because of their transitory living status.

Countries and economies are ranked in alphabetical order.

Coverage of the target population

Countries'/economies' sampling frames were required to cover at least 95% of the target population. The exclusion (non-coverage) of groups in the target population was expected to be limited to the greatest extent possible and to be based on operational or resource constraints, as in the case of populations located in remote and isolated regions. Countries/economies using population registers as sample frames could also treat untraceable individuals (i.e. individuals selected in the sample but who were not living at the registered address and could not be traced after multiple attempts) as exclusions, provided that the 5% threshold was not exceeded. All exclusions were required to be approved by the international consortium. Table 3.7 provides details of groups excluded from the sampling frame by design and the estimated proportion of the target population in the two categories of exclusions.

Sample size

The minimum sample size required for the Survey of Adult Skills depended on two variables: the number of cognitive domains assessed and the number of languages in which the assessment was administered. Participating countries/economies had the choice of assessing all three domains (literacy, numeracy and problem solving) or assessing literacy and numeracy only.

Table 3.8 **Sample size**

OECD countries and economies	Cognitive domains assessed	Assessment language(s)	Groups oversampled	Achieved Sample
Australia	L, N, PS-TRE	English	Persons resident in certain states and territories	7 428
Austria	L, N, PS-TRE	German		5 130
Canada	L, N, PS-TRE	English, French	Persons aged 16-25, provinces/territories, linguistic minorities, aboriginal persons, and recent immigrants	27 285
Chile	L, N, PS-TRE	Spanish		5 307
Czech Republic	L, N, PS-TRE	Czech	Persons aged 16-29	6 102
Denmark	L, N, PS-TRE	Danish	Persons aged 55-65, recent immigrants	7 328
England (UK)	L, N, PS-TRE	English		5 131
Estonia	L, N, PS-TRE	Estonian, Russian		7 632
Finland	L, N, PS-TRE	Finnish, Swedish		5 464
Flanders (Belgium)	L, N, PS-TRE	Dutch		5 463
France	L, N	French		6 993
Germany	L, N, PS-TRE	German		5 465
Greece	L, N, PS-TRE	Greek		4 925
Ireland	L, N, PS-TRE	English		5 983
Israel	L, N, PS-TRE	Hebrew, Arabic, Russian	The Arab population and Ultra-orthodox	5 538
Italy	L, N	Italian		4 621
Japan	L, N, PS-TRE	Japanese		5 278
Korea	L, N, PS-TRE	Korean		6 667
Netherlands	L, N, PS-TRE	Dutch		5 170
New Zealand	L, N, PS-TRE	English	Persons of Maori and Pacific ethnicities; persons aged 16-25	6 177
Northern Ireland (UK)	L, N, PS-TRE	English		3 761
Norway	L, N, PS-TRE	Norwegian		5 128
Poland	L, N, PS-TRE	Polish	Persons aged 19-26	9 366
Slovak Republic	L, N, PS-TRE	Slovak, Hungarian		5 723
Slovenia	L, N, PS-TRE	Slovenian		5 331
Spain	L, N	Castilian, Catalan, Basque, Galician, Valencian		6 055
Sweden	L, N, PS-TRE	Swedish		4 469
Turkey	L, N, PS-TRE	Turkish		5 277
United States	L, N, PS-TRE	English		5 010
Partners				
Cyprus[1]	L, N	Greek		5 053
Jakarta (Indonesia)	L, N	Indonesian		7 229
Lithuania	L, N, PS-TRE	Lithuanian		5 093
Russian Federation[2]	L, N, PS-TRE	Russian		3 892
Singapore	L, N, PS-TRE	English		5 468

Note: L = Literacy, N = Numeracy and PS-TRE = Problem Solving in Technology-Rich Environments.
1. See note 1 under Table 3.1.
2. See note at the end of this chapter.
Countries and economies are ranked in alphabetical order.

Assuming the assessment was administered in only one language, the minimum sample size required was 5 000 completed cases[4] if all three domains were assessed and 4 500 if only literacy and numeracy were assessed. If a country wished to fully report results in more than one language, the required sample size was either 4 500 or 5 000 cases per reporting language (e.g. 9 000 or 10 000 cases for two languages, depending on the domains assessed). If a country administered the assessment in more than one language but did not wish to report results separately by language, the sample size required was determined as follows: at least 5 000 (or 4 500) completed cases had to be collected in the principal language. The minimum number of completed cases in each of the additional languages was calculated in proportion to the estimated number of adults using the language. In other words, if 10% of the target population spoke a test language other than the principal language, the minimum required sample size was increased by 10%. A reduced sample was agreed for Northern Ireland (United Kingdom) to allow results to be reported separately from those of England (United Kingdom) for key variables.

Participating countries/economies were able to oversample particular subgroups of the target population if they wished to obtain more precise estimates of proficiency by geographical area (e.g. at the level of states or provinces) or for certain population groups (e.g. 16-24 year-olds or immigrants). A number of countries did so. Canada, for example, considerably increased the size of its sample to provide reliable estimates at the provincial and territorial level as well as oversampling persons aged 16-25, linguistic minorities, aboriginal population, and recent immigrants.

In addition, Australia and Denmark surveyed samples of individuals outside the survey target population. In the case of Australia, 15-year-olds and 66-74 year-olds were included as a supplemental sample. Chile also surveyed 15-year-olds. Denmark administered the assessment to individuals who had participated in PISA in 2000 and Singapore administered the assessment to individuals who had participated in PISA 2012. Results from individuals included in these national "supplemental samples" are not reported as part of the Survey of Adult Skills.

Table 3.8 provides information on the sample size by participating country, languages and oversampling.

Sample design

Participating countries/economies were required to use a probability sample representative of the target population. In other words, each individual in the target population had a calculable non-zero probability of being selected as part of the sample. In multi-stage sampling designs, each stage of the sampling process was required to be probability based. Non-probability designs, such as quota sampling and the random route approach, were not allowed at any sampling stage. Detailed information regarding sample designs can be found in the *Technical Report of the Survey of Adult Skills, Second Edition* (OECD, forthcoming).

TRANSLATION AND ADAPTATION OF INSTRUMENTS

Participating countries/economies were responsible for translating the assessment instruments and the background questionnaire. Any national adaptations of either the instruments or the questionnaire was subject to strict guidelines, and to review and approval by the international consortium. The recommended translation procedure was for a double translation from the English source version by two independent translators, followed by reconciliation by a third translator.

All national versions of the instruments were subject to a full verification before the field test, which involved:

- A sentence-by-sentence check of linguistic correctness, equivalence to the source version, and appropriateness of national adaptations.
- A final optical check to verify the final layout of the instruments, the equivalence of computer and paper forms, and the correct implementation of changes recommended by the verifiers.

All national version materials revised following the field test were subject to partial verification before the main study. Edits made between the field test and the main study were checked for their compliance with the PIAAC translation and adaptation guidelines and for correct implementation.

SURVEY ADMINISTRATION

The Survey of Adult Skills was administered under the supervision of trained interviewers either in the respondent's home or in a location agreed between the respondent and the interviewer. After the sampled person was identified, the survey was administered in two stages: completion of the background questionnaire and completion of the cognitive assessment.

The background questionnaire, which was the first part of the assessment, was administered in Computer-Aided Personal Interview format by the interviewer. Respondents were able to seek assistance from others in the household in completing the questionnaire, for example, in translating questions and answers. Proxy respondents were not permitted.

Following completion of the background questionnaire, the respondent undertook the cognitive assessment either using the computer provided by the interviewer or, by completing printed test booklets in the event that the respondent had limited computer skills, was estimated to have very low proficiency in literacy and numeracy, or opted not to take the test on the computer. Respondents were permitted to use technical aids such as an electronic calculator, a ruler (which were provided by interviewers) and to take notes or undertake calculations using a pen and pad during the assessment.

Respondents were not allowed to seek assistance from others in completing the cognitive assessment. However, the interviewer could intervene if the respondent had problems with the computer application or had questions on how to proceed with the assessment.

The direct-assessment component of the survey was not designed as a timed test; respondents could take as much or as little time as needed to complete it. However, interviewers were trained to encourage respondents to move to another section of the assessment if they were having difficulties. Respondents who started the cognitive assessment tended to finish it. The time taken to complete the cognitive assessment varied between 41 and 50 minutes on average depending on the country/language version.

The survey (background questionnaire plus cognitive assessment) was normally undertaken in one session. However, in exceptional circumstances, a respondent could take the questionnaire in one session and the cognitive assessment in another. The cognitive assessment was required to be completed in one session. Respondents who did not complete the assessment within a single session for whatever reason were not permitted to finish it at a later time.

Data collection in Round 1 of the Survey of Adult Skills took place from 1 August 2011 to 31 March 2012 in most participating countries/economies. In Canada, data collection took place from November 2011 to June 2012 and France collected data from September to November 2012. Data collection for Round 2 of the Survey of Adult Skills took place from 1 April 2014 to 31 March 2015.

Interviewers administering the survey were required to be trained according to common standards. These covered the timing and duration of training, its format and its content. A full set of training materials was provided to countries. The persons responsible for organising training nationally attended training sessions organised by the international consortium.

RESPONSE RATES AND NON-RESPONSE BIAS ANALYSIS

A major threat to the quality of the data produced by the Survey of Adult Skills was low response rates. The *PIAAC Technical Standards and Guidelines* (PIAAC, 2014) required that countries/economies put in place a range of strategies to reduce the incidence and effects of non-response, to adjust for it when it occurred, and to evaluate the effectiveness of any weighting adjustments implemented to reduce non-response bias. In particular, countries/economies were expected to establish procedures during data collection to minimise non-response. These included pre-collection publicity, selecting high-quality interviewers, delivering training on methods to reduce and convert refusals, and monitoring data collection closely to identify problem areas or groups and directing resources to these particular groups. At least seven attempts were to be made to contact a selected individual or household before it could be classed as a non-contact. The overall rate of non-contact was to be kept below 3%.

Response rates were calculated for each stage of the assessment: screener (only for countries/economies that need to sample households before selecting respondents); background questionnaire and Job Requirement Approach module; assessment (without reading components); and reading components.

The overall response rate was calculated as the product of the response rates (complete cases/eligible cases) for the relevant stages of the assessment. For countries/economies with a screener questionnaire, the overall response rate was the product of the response rates for the screener, background questionnaire/Job Requirement Approach module and assessment; for countries/economies without a screener, it was the product of the response rates for the questionnaire/module and the assessment.

The computations at each stage are hierarchical in that they depend on the response status from the previous data collection stage. A completed case thus involved completing the screener (if applicable), the background questionnaire, and the cognitive assessment. In the case of the questionnaire, a completed case was defined as having provided responses to key background questions, including age, gender, highest level of schooling and employment status or responses to age and gender for literacy-related non-respondents. For the cognitive assessment, a completed case was defined as having completed the "core" module, and a literacy/numeracy core module, or a case in which the core module was not completed for a literacy-related reason, for example, because of a language difficulty or because the respondent was unable to read or write in any of a country's test languages or because of learning or mental disability.

As noted above, countries/economies using population register-based sampling frames were able to treat some or all of the individuals in their samples who were untraceable as exclusions (i.e. as outside the target population) and exclude them from the numerator and denominator of the response-rate calculation (provided that the 5% threshold for exclusions was not exceeded).

The survey's *Technical Standards and Guidelines* set a goal of a 70% unit response rate. Seven countries achieved this goal, five in Round 1 and two in Round 2. For the most part, response rates were in the range of 50%-60%. Response rates by country/economy are presented in Table 3.9.

Table 3.9 **Achieved response rates and population coverage**

OECD countries and economies	Response rate	Coverage rate[3]
Australia	71	69
Austria	53	52
Canada	59	58
Chile	66	66
Czech Republic	66	65
Denmark	50	48
England (UK)	59	58
Estonia	63	61
Finland	66	66
Flanders (Belgium)	62	59
France	67	64
Germany	55	54
Greece	41	40
Ireland	72	72
Israel	61	58
Italy	55	54
Japan	50	47
Korea	75	73
Netherlands	51	50
New Zealand	63	61
Northern Ireland (UK)	65	64
Norway	62	62
Poland	56	53
Slovak Republic	66	63
Slovenia	62	59
Spain	48	46
Sweden	45	45
Turkey	80	79
United States	70	70
Partners		
Cyprus[1]	73	72
Jakarta (Indonesia)	82	unknown
Lithuania	54	53
Russian Federation[2]	52	51
Singapore	63	63

1. See note 1 under Table 3.1.
2. See note at the end of this chapter.
3. The coverage rate = response rate * (1 − rate of exclusions).
Countries and economies are ranked in alphabetical order.

Countries/economies worked to reduce non-response bias to the greatest extent possible before, during, and after data collection. Before data collection, countries implemented field procedures with the goal of obtaining a high level of co-operation. Most countries followed the PIAAC required sample monitoring activities to reduce bias to the lowest level possible during data collection. Finally, countries gathered and used auxiliary data to reduce bias in the outcome statistics through non-response adjustment weighting.

All countries/economies were required to conduct a basic non-response bias analysis (NRBA) and report the results. The basic analysis was used to evaluate the potential for bias and to select variables for non-response adjustment weighting. In addition, countries were required to conduct and report the results of a more extensive NRBA if the overall response rate was below 70%, or if any stage of data collection (screener, background questionnaire, or the assessment) response rate was below 80%. A NRBA was required for any BQ item with response rate below 85%.

Australia, Indonesia (Jakarta) Korea, Turkey and the United States achieved an overall response rate of 70% or greater. As their response rates for each stage were greater than 80%, they did not require the extended NRBA. Cyprus[1] and Ireland also achieved overall response rates of 70% or greater, but they achieved a lower than 80% response rate for one stage of their sample. The remaining countries achieved response rates lower than 70%.

The main purpose of the extended analysis was to assess the potential for remaining bias in the final weighted proficiency estimates after adjusting for non-response. As the proficiency levels of non-respondents are unknown, the NRBA is carried out by making assumptions about non-respondents. Multiple analyses were, therefore, undertaken to assess the potential for bias as each individual analysis has limitations due to the particular assumptions made about non-respondents. The extended NRBA included seven analyses (as listed below). Together, they were used to assess the patterns and potential for bias in each country data.

1. Comparison of estimates before and after weighting adjustments
2. Comparison of weighted estimates to external totals
3. Correlations of auxiliary variables and proficiency estimates
4. Comparison of estimates from alternative weighting adjustments
5. Analysis of variables collected during data collection
6. Level-of-effort analysis
7. Calculation of the range of potential bias

Cyprus[1] and Ireland were required to do only a subset of the analyses since their overall response rate was higher than 70%.

Table 3.10 **PIAAC NRBA outcome summary for countries/economies with response rates less than 70%**

OECD countries and economies	Outcome
Austria	Caution-Bias low
Canada	Caution-Bias minimal
Chile	Caution-Bias minimal
Czech Republic	Caution-Bias low
Denmark	Caution-Bias low
England (UK)	Caution-Bias unknown
Estonia	Caution-Bias low
Finland	Caution-Bias minimal
Flanders (Belgium)	Caution-Bias low
Germany	Caution-Bias low
Greece	Caution-Bias low
Israel	Caution-Bias minimal
Italy	Caution-Bias low
Japan	Caution-Bias low
Netherlands	Caution-Bias low
New Zealand	Caution-Bias minimal
Northern Ireland (UK)	Caution-Bias unknown
Norway	Caution-Bias low
Poland	Caution-Bias low
Slovak Republic	Caution-Bias low
Slovenia	Caution-Bias minimal
Spain	Caution-Bias low
Sweden	Caution-Bias low
Partners	
Lithuania	Caution-Bias low
Russian Federation[1]	Caution-Bias unknown
Singapore	Caution-Bias minimal

1. See note at the end of this chapter.
Countries and economies are ranked in alphabetical order.

Table 3.10 summarises the results of the NRBA for countries/economies with response rates lower than 70%. The overall conclusion was that, on the balance of evidence, the level of non-response bias was in the range of minimal to low in countries required to undertake the extended analysis available. The results for England/Northern Ireland (United Kingdom) were, however, inconclusive because many of the analyses were either incomplete or not conducted. Data users should be aware that the analyses are all based on various assumptions about non-respondents. Multiple analyses, with different assumptions, were included in the NRBA to protect against misleading results. However, the lower the response rate, the higher is the risk of hidden biases that are undetectable through non-response bias analysis even when multiple analyses are involved.

LITERACY-RELATED NON-RESPONSE

In most participating countries/economies a proportion of respondents were unable to undertake the assessment for literacy-related reasons, such as being unable to speak or read the test language(s), having difficulty reading or writing, or having a learning or mental disability. Some of these respondents completed the background questionnaire, or key parts of it, presumably with the assistance of an interviewer who spoke the respondent's language, a family member or another person.

Table 3.11 **Literacy-related non-response to the assessment: Proportion of respondents**

OECD countries and economies	Respondents with imputed scores (weighted %)	Respondents without imputed scores (literacy-related non response) (weighted %)
Australia	4.9	1.9
Austria	1.5	1.8
Canada	4.7	0.9
Chile	1.3	0.3
Czech Republic	0.3	0.6
Denmark	5.0	0.4
England/Northern Ireland (UK)	2.5	1.4
Estonia	1.7	0.4
Finland	6.1	0.0
Flanders (Belgium)	0.6	5.2
France	6.5	0.8
Germany	1.7	1.5
Greece	0.2	1.0
Ireland	3.3	0.5
Israel	1.7	2.4
Italy	3.9	0.7
Japan	0.1	1.2
Korea	2.2	0.3
Netherlands	1.7	2.3
New Zealand	0.2	1.9
Norway	4.6	2.2
Poland	1.1	0.0
Slovak Republic	1.6	0.3
Slovenia	0.3	0.6
Spain	2.0	0.8
Sweden	5.9	0.0
Turkey	2.4	2.0
United States	2.3	4.2
Partners		
Cyprus[1]	0.2	17.7
Jakarta (Indonesia)	0.5	0.0
Lithuania	0.1	4.5
Russian Federation[2]	0.0	0.0
Singapore	5.1	1.0

1. See note 1 under Table 3.1.
2. See note at the end of this chapter.
Countries and economies are ranked in alphabetical order.

The available background information regarding these respondents was used to impute proficiency scores in literacy and numeracy. Scores were not, however, imputed in problem solving in technology-rich environments domain, as these respondents did not undertake the ICT core assessment. Other respondents were able to provide only very limited background information as there was no one present (either the interviewer or another person) to translate into the language of the respondent or answer on behalf of the respondent. For most of these respondents, the only information collected was their age, gender and, in some cases, highest educational attainment. As a result, proficiency scores were not estimated for these respondents in any domain; however, they have been included as part of the weighted population totals and are included in the charts and tables in *OECD Skills Outlook 2013* (OECD, 2013) and *Skills Matter: Further Results from the Survey of Adult Skills* (OECD, 2016) under the category of literacy-related non-response (missing). The proportions of respondents who did not undertake the cognitive assessment and (a) received imputed scores and (b) did not receive imputed scores are presented in Table 3.11. Flanders (Belgium) and Cyprus[1] each stand out as having a high proportion of respondents who did not receive imputed scores due to having relatively high proportions of respondents for whom limited background information was available.

SCORING

For the large majority of respondents who took the assessment in its CBA format, scoring was done automatically. Manual scoring was necessary in the case of respondents taking the PBA version. Participating countries/economies were required to undertake within-country reliability studies during both the field test and main survey to check the consistency of scoring. This required a second scorer to re-score a pre-defined number of cognitive paper-and-pencil assessments.[5] The level of agreement between the two scorers was expected to be at least 95%.

Table 3.12 **Scoring of paper-based instruments: Within- and between-country agreement**

OECD countries and economies	Within-country agreement			Cross-country (anchor booklet) agreement		
	Core (%)	Literacy (%)	Numeracy (%)	Core (%)	Literacy (%)	Numeracy (%)
Australia	99.7	98.1	99.2	98.3	98.8	96.3
Austria	99.1	98.2	98.4	96.0	97.9	95.8
Canada	99.4	96.9	98.3	98.3	98.3	96.4
Chile	99.4	98.6	99.4	98.5	97.8	95.7
Czech Republic	100.0	99.6	100.0	98.3	97.2	96.5
Denmark	100.0	99.9	100.0	97.1	97.3	95.9
England/Northern Ireland (UK)	99.6	99.2	99.3	98.4	98.8	96.6
Estonia	99.8	96.4	98.9	95.5	95.5	95.5
Finland	99.3	98.4	98.8	97.5	98.4	96.1
Flanders (Belgium)	99.7	99.4	99.4	99.0	97.8	95.8
France	100.0	100.0	100.0	96.5	87.5	92.2
Germany	99.7	98.9	99.3	96.0	97.9	95.8
Greece	99.9	99.6	99.9	98.8	97.8	96.7
Ireland	99.4	96.2	96.7	97.1	96.7	95.0
Israel	99.4	98.7	98.9	98.8	98.2	96.8
Italy	99.9	99.8	99.7	97.9	97.0	96.2
Japan	100.0	100.0	100.0	99.2	97.9	97.0
Korea	99.5	99.9	99.9	98.8	99.1	96.7
Netherlands	99.0	97.5	98.5	95.6	92.1	95.5
New Zealand	99.7	98.9	99.4	98.6	97.8	96.6
Norway	99.6	98.2	98.7	96.6	96.5	95.9
Poland	100.0	100.0	100.0	99.0	97.3	96.0
Slovak Republic	99.9	99.8	99.9	99.6	95.0	96.1
Slovenia	99.5	97.4	99.1	98.3	97.8	96.6
Spain	99.5	97.9	98.7	97.7	96.3	95.7
Sweden	99.1	97.2	98.9	96.5	98.7	96.8
Turkey	98.9	96.8	98.4	98.3	95.6	96.1
United States	99.4	98.9	99.0	99.1	99.5	97.3
Partners						
Cyprus[1]	99.5	99.2	98.2	98.3	98.8	96.9
Jakarta (Indonesia)	99.3	96.3	98.3	97.1	92.9	94.9
Lithuania	99.7	98.7	99.6	97.9	97.3	96.1
Russian Federation[2]	100.0	100.0	100.0	94.0	86.7	91.5
Singapore	99.4	97.9	98.7	96.6	97.1	94.6

1. See note 1 under Table 3.1.
2. See note at the end of this chapter.
Countries and economies are ranked in alphabetical order.

In addition, a cross-country reliability study was conducted to identify the presence of systematic scoring bias across countries. At least two bilingual scorers (fluent in the national language and English) scored English-language international anchor booklets to ensure the equivalence of scoring across countries. These scores were compared and evaluated against the master scores for accuracy.

The levels of agreement achieved in the within-country and between-country studies of scoring reliability are presented in Table 3.12.

OVERALL ASSESSMENT OF DATA QUALITY

The data from participating countries/economies was subject to a process of "adjudication" to determine whether it was of sufficient quality to be reported and released to the public. The adjudication process used a broad definition of quality – that of "fitness for use". While countries' compliance with the requirements of the *PIAAC Technical Standards and Guidelines* (PIAAC, 2014) was an important component of the quality assessment, the goal was to go beyond compliance to assess whether the data produced were of sufficient quality in terms of their intended uses or applications. In assessing overall quality, the focus was on four key areas:

- sampling
- coverage and non-response bias
- data collection
- instrumentation.

In each of the domains identified above, countries/economies were assessed against a set of quality indicators. These indicators reflected the major requirements of the survey's *Technical Standards and Guidelines* (PIAAC, 2014) in the domains concerned. All countries/economies either fully met the required quality standards or, if they did not fully meet them, they met them to a degree that was believed not to compromise the overall quality of the data. The data from all participating countries/economies were determined to have met the quality standards required for reporting and public release. The assessments of the quality of participating countries' data were reviewed by the project's Technical Advisory Group before being submitted to the Board of Participating Countries.

In two countries, there were specific concerns about some aspects of the quality of data. These concerns and the action taken to rectify them are described below. In the Russian Federation, concerns regarding the process of data collection in the Moscow municipal area led to data from this area to be removed from the Russian data file. Thus, the sample for the Russian Federation covers the population of the Russian Federation with the exception of the population of the Moscow municipal area. In Greece, a large number of cases (1 032 in total) were collected without complete cognitive data. Proficiency scores in literacy and numeracy have been imputed for these cases. Further information can be found in the *Technical Report of the Survey of Adult Skills, Second Edition* (OECD, forthcoming).

Notes

1. See note regarding Cyprus under Table 3.1.

2. The exception was countries in which problem solving in technology-rich environments was not tested. In these cases, some respondents would take both a literacy and a numeracy module in CBA mode.

3. However, all respondents, whatever their characteristics and score on the core or the Stage 1 testlet, had some chance of being assigned to a testlet of a certain difficulty.

4. A completed case is defined as an interview in which the respondent provided answers to key background questions, including age, gender, highest level of schooling and employment status, and completed the "core" cognitive instrument (except in cases in which the respondent did not read the language[s] of the assessment).

5. In the main study, at least 600 cases (or 100% of cases if the number of respondents was less than 600) in each of the test languages had to be re-scored.

A note regarding the Russian Federation

The sample for the Russian Federation does not include the population of the Moscow municipal area. The data published, therefore, do not represent the entire resident population aged 16-65 in the Russian Federation but rather the population of the Russian Federation *excluding* the population residing in the Moscow municipal area.

More detailed information regarding the data from the Russian Federation as well as that of other countries can be found in the *Technical Report of the Survey of Adult Skills, Second Edition* (OECD, forthcoming).

References

OECD (forthcoming), *Technical Report of the Survey of Adult Skills, Second Edition*.

OECD (2013), *OECD Skills Outlook 2013: First Results from the Survey of Adult Skills*, OECD Publishing, Paris, http://dx.doi.org/10.1787/9789264204256-en.

PIAAC (2014), *PIAAC Technical Standards and Guidelines*, OECD Programme for the International Assessment of Adult Competencies, www.oecd.org/site/piaac/PIAAC-NPM%282014_06%29PIAAC_Technical_Standards_and_Guidelines.pdf.

4

Reporting the results of the Survey of Adult Skills (PIAAC)

This chapter examines the proficiency levels used to report the results of the Survey of Adult Skills (PIAAC). It provides information on the languages used and how results were reported in countries/economies that conducted the survey in more than one language.

This chapter describes how the results from the Survey of Adult Skills (PIAAC) are reported. It shows how the literacy, numeracy and problem-solving items used in the assessment are categorised according to their difficulty, the cognitive strategies required of adults to answer the questions, the real-life contexts in which such problems/questions may arise, and the medium used to deliver the item to the respondent. The chapter also shows how the proficiency levels for each of the three domains are related to the scores, and describes in detail what adults can do at each of the proficiency levels. The chapter concludes with information about the languages in which the test was conducted and the approach to reporting in countries/economies where the assessment was delivered in more than one language.

THE PROFICIENCY SCALES

In each of the three domains assessed, proficiency is considered as a *continuum of ability* involving the mastery of information-processing tasks of increasing complexity. The results are represented on a 500-point scale. At each point on the scale, an individual with a proficiency score of that particular value has a 67% chance of successfully completing test items located at that point.[1] This individual will also be able to complete more difficult items (those with higher values on the scale) with a lower probability of success and easier items (those with lower values on the scale) with a greater chance of success.

To illustrate this point, Table 4.1 shows the probability with which a person with a proficiency score of 300 on the literacy scale can successfully complete items of greater and lesser difficulty. As can be seen, a person with a proficiency score of 300 will successfully complete items of this level of difficulty 67% of the time, items with a difficulty value of 250, 95% of the time, and items with a difficulty value of 350, 28% of the time.

Table 4.1 **Probability of successfully completing items of varying difficulty for a person scoring 300 on the literacy scale**

	Difficulty score (literacy scale)			
	200	**250**	**300**	**350**
Probability of success	0.97	0.95	0.67	0.28

PROFICIENCY LEVELS

The proficiency scale in each of the domains assessed can be described in relation to the items that are located at the different points on the scale according to their difficulty. Tables 4.2, 4.3 and 4.4 present the location of the test items used in the Survey of Adult Skills on the difficult scales in the three domains assessed. In addition to the difficulty score, unit name and ID, a description of the key features of the item is provided in relation to the relevant measurement framework.

To help interpret the results, the reporting scales have been divided into "proficiency levels" defined by particular score-point ranges. Six proficiency levels are defined for literacy and numeracy (Levels 1 through 5 plus below Level 1) and four for problem solving in technology-rich environments (Levels 1 through 3 plus below Level 1). These descriptors provide a summary of the characteristics of the types of tasks that can be successfully completed by adults with proficiency scores in a particular range. In other words, they offer a summary of what adults with particular proficiency scores in a particular skill domain can do.

With the exception of the lowest level (below Level 1), tasks located at a particular level can be successfully completed approximately 50% of the time by a person with a proficiency score at the bottom of the range defining the level. In other words, a person with a score at the bottom of Level 2 would score close to 50% in a test made up of items of Level 2 difficulty. A person at the top of the level will get items located at that level correct most of the time. The "average" individual with a proficiency score in the range defining a level will successfully complete items located at that level approximately two-thirds of the time.

Table 4.2 [1/2] **Literacy item map**

Difficulty score	Unit name	Item ID	Cognitive strategies	Context	Medium	Format
			CBA/PBA Design			
376	Library Search	C323P005	Evaluate and reflect	Education and training	Digital	Multiple
374	Work-related Stress	C329P003	Integrate and interpret	Work-related	Digital	Multiple
372	CANCO	C306B111	Access and identify	Work-related	Print	Continuous
371	Baltic Stock Market	C308A116	Access and identify	Personal	Print	Mixed
359	Apples	P317P001	Integrate and interpret	Personal	Print	Continuous
350	Summer Streets	C327P004	Evaluate and reflect	Community	Digital	Mixed
349	Work-related Stress	C329P002	Evaluate and reflect	Work-related	Digital	Multiple
348	Library Search	C323P002	Integrate and interpret	Education and training	Digital	Multiple
347	Milk Label	P324P002	Integrate and interpret	Personal	Print	Mixed
337	Baltic Stock Market	C308A118	Access and identify	Personal	Print	Mixed
329	Generic Medicines	C309A322	Integrate and interpret	Personal	Print	Mixed
329	Library Search	C323P004	Evaluate and reflect	Education and training	Digital	Multiple
324	International Calls	C313A410	Access and identify	Personal	Print	Mixed
320	Summer Streets	C327P003	Integrate and interpret	Community	Digital	Mixed
318	Distances-Mexican Cities	C315B512	Integrate and interpret	Community	Print	Non-continuous
316	Civil Engineering	C318P003	Integrate and interpret	Education and training	Digital	Mixed
315	International Calls	C313A411	Access and identify	Personal	Print	Mixed
312	Memory Training	C310A407	Integrate and interpret	Personal	Print	Continuous
312	Milk Label	P324P003	Access and identify	Personal	Print	Mixed
309	TMN Anti-Theft	C305A218	Integrate and interpret	Community	Print	Continuous
306	Summer Streets	C327P002	Evaluate and reflect	Community	Digital	Mixed
304	Contact Employer	C304B711	Integrate and interpret	Work-related	Print	Continuous
303	Civil Engineering	C318P001	Access and identify	Education and training	Digital	Mixed
298	Summer Streets	C327P001	Integrate and interpret	Community	Digital	Mixed
297	Baltic Stock Market	C308A119	Access and identify	Personal	Print	Mixed
294	Lakeside Fun Run	C322P003	Access and identify	Personal	Digital	Mixed
293	Lakeside Fun Run	C322P004	Access and identify	Personal	Digital	Mixed
289	Library Search	C323P003	Access and identify	Education and training	Digital	Multiple
288	MEDCO Aspirin	C307B402	Access and identify	Personal	Print	Continuous
286	Contact Employer	C304B710	Access and identify	Work-related	Print	Continuous
286	International Calls	C313A413	Access and identify	Personal	Print	Mixed
286	Discussion forum	C320P003	Evaluate and reflect	Work-related	Digital	Multiple
285	Discussion forum	C320P004	Evaluate and reflect	Work-related	Digital	Multiple
283	Lakeside Fun Run	C322P001	Integrate and interpret	Personal	Digital	Mixed
281	Discussion forum	C320P001	Integrate and interpret	Work-related	Digital	Multiple
279	Baltic Stock Market	C308A121	Access and identify	Personal	Print	Mixed
272	Generic Medicines	C309A319	Access and identify	Personal	Print	Mixed
272	Memory Training	C310A406	Access and identify	Personal	Print	Continuous
272	International Calls	C313A414	Access and identify	Personal	Print	Mixed
265	Apples	P317P003	Evaluate and reflect	Personal	Print	Continuous
262	Apples	P317P002	Integrate and interpret	Personal	Print	Continuous
260	TMN Anti-theft	C305A215	Access and identify	Community	Print	Continuous
257	International Calls	C313A412	Access and identify	Personal	Print	Mixed
254	Baltic Stock Market	C308A120	Access and identify	Personal	Print	Mixed
251	Internet Poll	C321P001	Integrate and interpret	Community	Digital	Multiple
244	CANCO	C306B110	Access and identify	Work-related	Print	Continuous
244	Lakeside Fun Run	C322P005	Access and identify	Personal	Digital	Mixed
240	Lakeside Fun Run	C322P002	Evaluate and reflect	Personal	Digital	Mixed
239	Baltic Stock Market	C308A117	Access and identify	Personal	Print	Mixed
239	Generic Medicines	C309A320	Access and identify	Personal	Print	Mixed
238	Internet Poll	C321P002	Access and identify	Community	Digital	Multiple
219	Generic Medicines	C309A321	Integrate and interpret	Personal	Print	Mixed
207	Guadeloupe	P330P001	Access and identify	Community	Print	Mixed
201	Dutch Women	C311B701	Access and identify	Community	Print	Mixed
169	MEDCO Aspirin	C30B7401	Access and identify	Personal	Print	Continuous
162	Election Results	C302BC02	Access and identify	Community	Print	Mixed
136	Employment Ad	C300AC02	Access and identify	Work-related	Print	Continuous
75	SGIH	C301AC05	Access and identify	Community	Print	Non-continuous

Note: CBA = computer-based assessment; PBA = paper-based assessment.   ...

Table 4.2 [2/2] **Literacy item map**

Difficulty score	Unit name	Item ID	Cognitive strategies	Context	Medium	Format
			PBA ONLY (Indonesia [Jakarta])			
385	CANCO	P306B111	Integrate and interpret	Work-related	Digital	Multiple
374	Water Chlorination	P340A426	Access and identify	Community	Print	Continuous
347	Milk Label	P324P002	Evaluate and reflect	Education	Digital	Multiple
337	Baltic Stock Market	P308A118	Access and identify	Personal	Print	Mixed
331	Water Chlorination	P340A424	Integrate	Community	Print	Continuous
329	Apples	P317P001	Integrate and interpret	Community	Print	Non-continuous
329	Generic Medicine	P309A322	Evaluate and reflect	Community	Digital	Mixed
320	International Calls	P313A411	Access and identify	Community	Print	Mixed
318	Mexican Cities	P315B512	Integrate and interpret	Community	Print	Non-continuous
317	International Calls	P313A410	Integrate and interpret	Personal	Print	Mixed
312	Memory Training	P310A407	Integrate and interpret	Personal	Print	Continuous
312	Milk Label	P324P003	Evaluate and reflect	Education	Digital	Multiple
301	Water Chlorination	P340A422	Access and identify	Community	Print	Continuous
297	Baltic Stock Market	P308A119	Integrate and interpret	Personal	Print	Mixed
295	Baltic Stock Market	P308A116	Access and identify	Personal	Print	Mixed
291	International Calls	P313A413	Access and identify	Personal	Print	Mixed
288	MEDCO Aspirin	P307B402	Access and identify	Personal	Print	Mixed
281	Preschool Rules	P303A103	Access and identify	Personal	Print	Mixed
281	Generic Medicine	P309A319	Access and identify	Personal	Digital	Mixed
267	Generic Medicine	P309A321	Evaluate and reflect	Education and training	Digital	Multiple
265	Exercise Equipment	P312A315	Access and identify	Personal	Digital	Mixed
265	Apples	P317P003	Integrate and interpret	Community	Print	Non-continuous
262	Apples	P317P002	Integrate and interpret	Community	Print	Non-continuous
260	TMN AntiTheft	P305A215	Access and identify	Personal	Print	Mixed
255	Swimmer Completes	P341B502	Access and identify	Community	Print	Continuous
255	Problem Solver	P314B101	Access and identify	Personal	Digital	Mixed
254	Baltic Stock Market	P308A120	Access and identify	Personal	Print	Continuous
253	International Calls	P313A412	Access and identify	Personal	Print	Mixed
250	TMN AntiTheft	P305A218	Access and identify	Personal	Print	Mixed
247	International Calls	P313A414	Access and identify	Personal	Print	Mixed
246	Memory Training	P310A406	Evaluate and reflect	Work-related	Digital	Multiple
245	Exercise Equipment	P312A318	Access and identify	Personal	Digital	Mixed
239	Baltic Stock Market	P308A117	Access and identify	Personal	Print	Mixed
235	CANCO	P306B110	Access and identify	Education and training	Digital	Mixed
234	Problem Solver	P314B102	Access and identify	Personal	Digital	Mixed
231	Preschool Rules	P303A102	Access and identify	Personal	Print	Continuous
219	Generic Medicine	P309A320	Access and identify	Education and training	Digital	Multiple
169	MEDCO Aspirin	P307B401	Access and indentify	Work-related	Print	Continuous
162	Election Results	P302BC02	Integrate and interpret	Personal	Print	Continuous
149	Swimmer Completes	P341B501	Access and identify	Community	Print	Continuous
140	Guadeloupe	P330P001	Integrate and interpret	Work-related	Digital	Multiple
136	Employment Ad.	P300AC02	Integrate and interpret	Personal	Print	Mixed
75	SGIH	P301AC05	Access and identify	Personal	Print	Continuous

Note: PBA = paper-based assessment.

Table 4.3 [1/2] **Numeracy item map**

Difficulty score	Unit name	Item ID	Content	Cognitive strategies	Context
	CBA/PBA Design				
375	Dioxin (MOD)	C612A518	Pattern, relationships, change	Interpret, evaluate	Community and society
354	Educational Level	C632P001	Data and chance	Interpret, evaluate	Community and society
348	Compound Interest	P610A515	Pattern, relationships, change	Act upon, use	Education and training
341	Wine	P623A618	Data and chance	Interpret, evaluate	Community and society
332	Weight history	C660P004	Pattern, relationships, change	Act upon, use	Community and society
326	Cooper test	C665P002	Pattern, relationships, change	Act upon, use	Everyday life
324	Amoeba	C641P001	Pattern, relationships, change	Act upon, use	Education and training
320	BMI	C624A620	Pattern, relationships, change	Act upon, use	Everyday life
318	Peanuts	C634P002	Pattern, relationships, change	Act upon, use	Everyday life
317	NZ Exports	C644P002	Pattern, relationships, change	Act upon, use	Community and society
315	Study fees	C661P002	Data and chance	Interpret, evaluate	Community and society
315	Package	C657P001	Dimension and shape	Interpret, evaluate	Work-related
314	Fertilizer	C651P002	Pattern, relationships, change	Interpret, evaluate	Work-related
308	Study fees	C661P001	Data and chance	Interpret, evaluate	Community and society
308	Inflation	C620A612	Data and chance	Act upon, use	Community and society
307	Orchestra tickets	C664P001	Pattern, relationships, change	Act upon, use	Work-related
305	Peanuts	C634P001	Pattern, relationships, change	Act upon, use	Everyday life
303	Map	C617A605	Dimension and shape	Interpret, evaluate	Work-related
301	Classified	C622A615	Pattern, relationships, change	Act upon, use	Work-related
297	SixPack1	C618A608	Quantity and number	Act upon, use	Education and training
296	Temp Scale	C611A517	Dimension and shape	Interpret, evaluate	Community and society
294	Lab Report	C636P001	Quantity and number	Interpret, evaluate	Everyday life
287	Map	C617A606	Dimension and shape	Act upon, use	Work-related
282	Tiles	C619A609	Dimension and shape	Act upon, use	Everyday life
276	Wine	C623A617	Quantity and number	Act upon, use	Community and society
276	Weight history	C660P003	Data and chance	Interpret, evaluate	Everyday life
273	Solution	C606A509	Dimension and shape	Act upon, use	Work-related
267	Inflation	C620A610	Data and chance	Identify, locate or access	Community and society
266	Educational Level	C632P002	Data and chance	Interpret, evaluate	Community and society
261	Temp Scale	C611A516	Dimension and shape	Interpret, evaluate	Community and society
260	Urban Population	C650P001	Data and chance	Interpret, evaluate	Community and society
260	Tree	C608A513	Dimension and shape	Act upon, use	Everyday life
259	Photo	C605A506	Dimension and shape	Act upon, use	Everyday life
259	Price Tag	C602A503	Quantity and number	Act upon, use	Everyday life
258	Wine	C623A616	Quantity and number	Act upon, use	Community and society
256	Rug Production	C646P002	Data and chance	Act upon, use	Community and society
250	Logbook	C613A520	Pattern, relationships, change	Act upon, use	Work-related
249	Path	C655P001	Pattern, relationships, change	Act upon, use	Everyday life
242	Photo	C605A507	Dimension and shape	Interpret, evaluate	Everyday life
240	Rope	P666P001	Dimension and shape	Act upon, use	Work-related
239	TV	C607A510	Pattern, relationships, change	Act upon, use	Everyday life
238	Price Tag	C602A502	Quantity and number	Act upon, use	Everyday life
234	Cooper test	C665P001	Data and chance	Interpret, evaluate	Everyday life
231	Candles	C615A603	Dimension and shape	Act upon, use	Work-related
231	Airport Timetable	C645P001	Dimension and shape	Act upon, use	Work-related
228	Gas Gauge	C604A505	Quantity and number	Act upon, use	Everyday life
227	Photo	C605A508	Quantity and number	Act upon, use	Everyday life
221	BMI	C624A619	Data and chance	Identify, locate or access	Everyday life
221	Candles	C615A602	Dimension and shape	Interpret, evaluate	Education and training
217	SixPack1	C618A607	Quantity and number	Act upon, use	Everyday life
195	Odometer	P640P001	Dimension and shape	Act upon, use	Everyday life
185	Watch	C614A601	Quantity and number	Interpret, evaluate	Everyday life
179	Parking Map	C635P001	Dimension and shape	Identify, locate or access	Work-related
168	Price Tag	C602A501	Quantity and number	Act upon, use	Everyday life
155	Election results	C600AC04	Quantity and number	Act upon, use	Work-related
129	Bottles	C601AC06	Dimension and Shape	Interpret, evaluate	Everyday life
136	Employment Ad	C300AC02	Access and identify	Work-related	Print
75	SGIH	C301AC05	Access and identify	Community	Print

Note: CBA = computer-based assessment; PBA = paper-based assessment.

...

Table 4.3 [2/2] **Numeracy item map**

Difficulty score	Unit name	Item ID	Content	Cognitive strategies	Context
PBA ONLY (Indonesia [Jakarta])					
348	CompoundInteres	P610A515	Pattern, relationships, change	Act upon, use	Further learning
341	Wine	P623A618	Data and chance	Interpret, evaluate	Community and society
332	Weighthistory	P660P004	Pattern, relationships, change	Act upon, use	Everyday life
328	TempScale	P611A517	Dimension and Shape	Interpret, evaluate	Community and society
320	BMI	P624A620	Pattern, relationships, change	Act upon, use	Everyday life
318	Peanuts	P634P002	Pattern, relationships, change	Act upon, use	Everyday life
314	Fertilizer	P651P002	Pattern, relationships, change	Interpret, evaluate	Workplace
308	Inflation	P620A612	Data and chance	Act upon, use	Community and society
305	Peanuts	P634P001	Pattern, relationships, change	Act upon, use	Everyday life
301	Classified	P622A615	Pattern, relationships, change	Act upon, use	Workplace
301	Orchestraticket	P664P001	Pattern, relationships, change	Act upon, use	Workplace
294	LabReport	P636P001	Quantity and number	Interpret, evaluate	Everyday life
286	Package	P657P001	Dimension and Shape	Interpret, evaluate	Workplace
282	Tiles	P619A609	Dimension and Shape	Act upon, use	Everyday life
281	TempScale	P611A516	Dimension and Shape	Interpret, evaluate	Community and society
276	Wine	P623A617	Quantity and number	Act upon, use	Community and society
276	Weighthistory	P660P003	Data and chance	Interpret, evaluate	Everyday life
273	Solution	P606A509	Dimension and Shape	Act upon, use	Workplace
267	Inflation	P620A610	Data and chance	Identify, locate or access	Community and society
260	UrbanPopulation	P650P001	Data and chance	Interpret, evaluate	Community and society
260	Tree	P608A513	Dimension and Shape	Act upon, use	Everyday life
258	Wine	P623A616	Quantity and number	Act upon, use	Community and society
258	SixPack1	P618A608	Quantity and number	Act upon, use	Further learning
252	PriceTag	P602A503	Quantity and number	Act upon, use	Everyday life
250	Logbook	P613A520	Pattern, relationships, change	Act upon, use	Workplace
248	Parking Time	P616A604	Dimension and Shape	Interpret, evaluate	Workplace
241	Path	P655P001	Pattern, relationships, change	Act upon, use	Everyday life
240	Rope	P666P001	Dimension and Shape	Act upon, use	Workplace
239	TV	P607A510	Pattern, relationships, change	Act upon, use	Everyday life
231	Candles	P615A603	Dimension and Shape	Act upon, use	Workplace
228	GasGauge	P604A505	Quantity and number	Act upon, use	Everyday life
226	PriceTag	P602A502	Quantity and number	Act upon, use	Everyday life
223	Airport Timetab	P645P001	Dimension and Shape	Act upon, use	Everyday life
221	Craft	P621A613	Quantity and number	Act upon, use	Further learning
221	BMI	P624A619	Data and chance	Identify, locate or access	Everyday life
221	Candles	P615A602	Dimension and Shape	Interpret, evaluate	Further learning
197	Raincoat	P603A504	Pattern, relationships, change	Act upon, use	Everyday life
195	Odometer	P640P001	Dimension and Shape	Act upon, use	Everyday life
178	Watch	P614A601	Quantity and number	Interpret, evaluate	Everyday life
168	PriceTag	P602A501	Quantity and number	Act upon, use	Everyday life
165	SixPack1	P618A607	Quantity and number	Act upon, use	Everyday life
155	Election Result	P600AC04	Quantity and number	Act upon, use	Everyday life
127	Bottles	P601AC06	Dimension and Shape	Interpret, evaluate	Everyday life

Note: PBA = paper-based assessment.

Table 4.4 [1/2] **Problem solving in technology-rich environments item map**

Difficulty score	Item name	Item ID	Content Technology	Content Task	Cognitive strategies	Context	Description
374	Class Attendance	U04A	Spread-sheet, e-mail	• Multiple steps • Single constraint • Explicit problem statement	• Goal setting and progress monitoring • Planning, self-organising • Acquiring and evaluating information • Making use of information	Work-related	Using information embedded in an e-mail message, establish and apply the criteria to transform the e-mail information to a spreadsheet. Monitor the progress of correctly organising information to perform computations through novel built-in functions.
355	Locate E-mail – File 3 e-mails	U11B	E-mail	• Single step • Single constraint • Implicit problem statement	• Goal setting and progress monitoring • Planning, self-organising • Acquiring and evaluating information • Making use of information	Personal	Infer the proper folder destination in order to transfer a subset of incoming e-mail messages based on the subject header and the specific contents of each message.
346	Meeting Rooms	U02	E-mail, Internet	• Multiple steps • Multiple constraints • Implicit problem statement	• Goal setting and progress monitoring • Planning, self-organising • Acquiring and evaluating information • Making use of information	Work-related	Using information from a novel Internet application and several e-mail messages, establish and apply criteria to solve a scheduling problem where an impasse must be resolved, and communicate the outcome.
342	Sprained Ankle – Site Evaluation Table	U06A	Internet	• Single step • Single constraint • Explicit problem statement	• Acquiring and evaluating information	Personal	Evaluate several entries in a search engine results page given an explicit set of separate reliability criteria.
325	Sprained Ankle – Reliable/ Trustworthy Site	U06B	Internet	• Multiple steps • Single constraint • Explicit problem statement	• Goal setting and progress monitoring • Acquiring and evaluating information • Making use of information	Personal	Apply evaluation criteria and then navigate through multiple websites to infer the most reliable and trustworthy site. Monitoring throughout the process is required.
320	Tickets	U21	Internet	• Multiple steps • Multiple constraints • Explicit problem statement	• Goal setting and progress monitoring • Planning, self-organising • Acquiring and evaluating information	Personal	Use a novel Internet-based application involving multiple tools to complete an order based on a combination of explicit criteria.
321	Lamp Return	U23	Internet, e-mail	• Multiple steps • Single constraint • Explicit problem statement	• Goal setting and progress monitoring • Planning, self-organising • Acquiring and evaluating information	Personal	Enact a plan to navigate through a website to complete an explicitly specified consumer transaction. Monitor the progress of submitting a request, retrieving an e-mail message, and filling out a novel online form.

...

Table 4.4 [2/2] **Problem solving in technology-rich environments item map**

Difficulty score	Item name	Item ID	Content		Cognitive strategies	Context	Description
			Technology	Task			
316	CD Tally	U03A	Internet, spreadsheet	• Single step • Single constraint • Implicit problem statement	• Goal setting and progress monitoring • Planning, self-organising • Making use of information	Work-related	Organise large amounts of information in a multiple column spreadsheet and determine a value based on a single explicit criterion; use a drop-down menu in a novel Internet application to communicate the result.
305	Digital Photography Book Purchase	U07	Internet	• Multiple steps • Multiple constraints • Implicit problem statement	• Goal setting and progress monitoring • Acquiring and evaluating information	Work-related	Choose an item on a web page that best matches a set of given criteria from a search engine results page; the information can be made available only by clicking on links and navigating through several web pages; based on a search engine results page, navigate through several Internet sites in order to choose an item on a web page that best matches a set of given criteria.
299	Party Invitations Accommodations	U01B	E-mail	• Single step • Multiple constraints • Implicit problem statement	• Planning, self-organising • Making use of information	Personal	Categorise a small number of messages in an e-mail application by creating a new folder; evaluate the contents of the entries based on one criterion in order to file them in the proper folder.
296	Club Membership – Eligibility for Club President	U19B	Spreadsheet, e-mail	• Single step • Multiple constraints • Implicit problem statement	• Goal setting and progress monitoring • Planning, self-organising • Acquiring and evaluating information • Making use of information	Society-community	Organise large amounts of information in a multiple-column spreadsheet using multiple explicit criteria; locate and mark relevant entries.
286	Party Invitations – Can/Cannot Come	U01A	E-mail	• Single step • Single constraint • Implicit problem statement	• Planning, self-organising • Making use of information	Personal	Categorise a small number of messages in an e-mail application into existing folders according to one explicit criterion.
286	Reply All	U16	E-mail	• Single step • Single constraint • Explicit problem statement	• Acquiring and evaluating information • Planning, self-organising	Personal	With a defined goal and explicit criteria, use e-mail and send information to three people.
268	Club Membership – Member ID	U19A	Spreadsheet, e-mail	• Single step • Single constraint • Implicit problem statement	• Planning, self-organising • Acquiring and evaluating information	Society-community	Locate an item within a large amount of information in a multiple-column spreadsheet based on a single explicit criterion; use e-mail to communicate the result.

THE SURVEY OF ADULT SKILLS: READER'S COMPANION, SECOND EDITION

Literacy and numeracy

Six proficiency levels are defined for the domains of literacy and numeracy. The score-point ranges defining each level and the descriptors of the characteristics of tasks located at each of the levels can be found in Table 4.5. In the case of literacy and numeracy, the score-point ranges associated with each proficiency level are the same as those that apply in the International Adult Literacy Survey (IALS) and the Adult Literacy and Life Skills Survey (ALL) for document and prose literacy and in ALL for numeracy. However, the descriptors that apply to the proficiency levels in the domains of literacy and numeracy differ between the Survey of Adult Skills (PIAAC) and IALS and ALL.

Table 4.5 [1/2] **Proficiency levels: Literacy and numeracy**

Level	Score range	Literacy	Numeracy
Below Level 1	Below 176 points	The tasks at this level require the respondent to read brief texts on familiar topics to locate a single piece of specific information. There is seldom any competing information in the text and the requested information is identical in form to information in the question or directive. The respondent may be required to locate information in short continuous texts. However, in this case, the information can be located as if the text was non-continuous in format. Only basic vocabulary knowledge is required, and the reader is not required to understand the structure of sentences or paragraphs or make use of other text features. Tasks below Level 1 do not make use of any features specific to digital texts.	Tasks at this level require the respondents to carry out simple processes such as counting, sorting, performing basic arithmetic operations with whole numbers or money, or recognising common spatial representations in concrete, familiar contexts where the mathematical content is explicit with little or no text or distractors.
1	176 to less than 226 points	Most of the tasks at this level require the respondent to read relatively short digital or print continuous, non-continuous, or mixed texts to locate a single piece of information that is identical to or synonymous with the information given in the question or directive. Some tasks, such as those involving non-continuous texts, may require the respondent to enter personal information onto a document. Little, if any, competing information is present. Some tasks may require simple cycling through more than one piece of information. Knowledge and skill in recognising basic vocabulary determining the meaning of sentences, and reading paragraphs of text is expected.	Tasks at this level require the respondent to carry out basic mathematical processes in common, concrete contexts where the mathematical content is explicit with little text and minimal distractors. Tasks usually require one-step or simple processes involving counting; sorting; performing basic arithmetic operations; understanding simple percentages such as 50%; and locating and identifying elements of simple or common graphical or spatial representations.
2	226 to less than 276 points	At this level, the medium of texts may be digital or printed, and texts may comprise continuous, non-continuous, or mixed types. Tasks at this level require respondents to make matches between the text and information, and may require paraphrasing or low-level inferences. Some competing pieces of information may be present. Some tasks require the respondent to • cycle through or integrate two or more pieces of information based on criteria; • compare and contrast or reason about information requested in the question; or • navigate within digital texts to access-and-identify information from various parts of a document.	Tasks at this level require the respondent to identify and act on mathematical information and ideas embedded in a range of common contexts where the mathematical content is fairly explicit or visual with relatively few distractors. Tasks tend to require the application of two or more steps or processes involving calculation with whole numbers and common decimals, percentages and fractions; simple measurement and spatial representation; estimation; and interpretation of relatively simple data and statistics in texts, tables and graphs.
3	276 to less than 326 points	Texts at this level are often dense or lengthy, and include continuous, non-continuous, mixed, or multiple pages of text. Understanding text and rhetorical structures become more central to successfully completing tasks, especially navigating complex digital texts. Tasks require the respondent to identify, interpret, or evaluate one or more pieces of information, and often require varying levels of inference. Many tasks require the respondent to construct meaning across larger chunks of text or perform multi-step operations in order to identify and formulate responses. Often tasks also demand that the respondent disregard irrelevant or inappropriate content to answer accurately. Competing information is often present, but it is not more prominent than the correct information.	Tasks at this level require the respondent to understand mathematical information that may be less explicit, embedded in contexts that are not always familiar and represented in more complex ways. Tasks require several steps and may involve the choice of problem-solving strategies and relevant processes. Tasks tend to require the application of number sense and spatial sense; recognising and working with mathematical relationships, patterns, and proportions expressed in verbal or numerical form; and interpretation and basic analysis of data and statistics in texts, tables and graphs.

...

Table 4.5 [2/2] **Proficiency levels: Literacy and numeracy**

Level	Score range	Literacy	Numeracy
4	326 to less than 376 points	Tasks at this level often require respondents to perform multiple-step operations to integrate, interpret, or synthesise information from complex or lengthy continuous, non-continuous, mixed, or multiple type texts. Complex inferences and application of background knowledge may be needed to perform the task successfully. Many tasks require identifying and understanding one or more specific, non-central idea(s) in the text in order to interpret or evaluate subtle evidence-claim or persuasive discourse relationships. Conditional information is frequently present in tasks at this level and must be taken into consideration by the respondent. Competing information is present and sometimes seemingly as prominent as correct information.	Tasks at this level require the respondent to understand a broad range of mathematical information that may be complex, abstract or embedded in unfamiliar contexts. These tasks involve undertaking multiple steps and choosing relevant problem-solving strategies and processes. Tasks tend to require analysis and more complex reasoning about quantities and data; statistics and chance; spatial relationships; and change, proportions and formulas. Tasks at this level may also require understanding arguments or communicating well-reasoned explanations for answers or choices.
5	Equal to or higher than 376 points	At this level, tasks may require the respondent to search for and integrate information across multiple, dense texts; construct syntheses of similar and contrasting ideas or points of view; or evaluate evidence-based arguments. Application and evaluation of logical and conceptual models of ideas may be required to accomplish tasks. Evaluating reliability of evidentiary sources and selecting key information is frequently a requirement. Tasks often require respondents to be aware of subtle, rhetorical cues and to make high-level inferences or use specialised background knowledge.	Tasks at this level require the respondent to understand complex representations and abstract and formal mathematical and statistical ideas, possibly embedded in complex texts. Respondents may have to integrate multiple types of mathematical information where considerable translation or interpretation is required; draw inferences; develop or work with mathematical arguments or models; and justify, evaluate and critically reflect upon solutions or choices.

This is because the domain of *literacy* in the Survey of Adult Skills replaces the previously separate domains of prose and document literacy used in IALS and ALL, and because the survey defines proficiency levels differently than the other surveys do. An explanation of these changes and their impact is provided in Annex A.

Tables 4.6 and 4.7 show the probability that adults with particular proficiency scores will complete items of different levels of difficulty in the domains of literacy and numeracy. For example, an adult with a proficiency score of 300 in literacy (i.e. the mid-point of Level 3) has a 68% chance of successfully completing items of Level 3 difficulty. He or she has a 29% chance of completing items of Level 4 difficulty and a 90% probability of successfully completing items of Level 2 difficulty.

Table 4.6 **Probability of successfully completing items at different difficulty levels, by proficiency score: Literacy**

Item difficulty	Proficiency score											
	150	175	200	225	250	275	300	325	350	375	400	425
Level 1	0.56	0.68	0.78	0.86	0.92	0.95	0.97	0.98	0.99	0.99	1.00	1.00
Level 2	0.08	0.15	0.27	0.44	0.63	0.80	0.90	0.95	0.98	0.99	0.99	1.00
Level 3	0.01	0.03	0.06	0.13	0.26	0.46	0.68	0.83	0.92	0.96	0.98	0.99
Level 4	0.01	0.01	0.02	0.05	0.09	0.16	0.29	0.47	0.65	0.80	0.90	0.95

Table 4.7 **Probability of successfully completing items at different difficulty levels, by proficiency score: Numeracy**

Item difficulty	Proficiency score											
	150	175	200	225	250	275	300	325	350	375	400	425
Level 1	0.47	0.60	0.72	0.82	0.89	0.93	0.96	0.98	0.99	0.99	1.00	1.00
Level 2	0.11	0.20	0.33	0.49	0.66	0.80	0.89	0.94	0.97	0.98	0.99	1.00
Level 3	0.02	0.04	0.08	0.15	0.26	0.43	0.63	0.80	0.90	0.95	0.98	0.99
Level 4	0.02	0.03	0.05	0.08	0.14	0.24	0.37	0.54	0.69	0.80	0.88	0.93

  THE SURVEY OF ADULT SKILLS: READER'S COMPANION, SECOND EDITION

Problem solving in technology-rich environments

The problem-solving proficiency scale was divided into four levels. The problem solving in technology-rich environments framework (PIAAC Problem Sloving in Technology-Rich Environment, 2009) identifies three main dimensions along which problems vary in quality and complexity. These are (1) the technology dimension, (2) the task dimension and (3) the cognitive dimension. Variations along each of these dimensions contribute to the overall difficulty of a problem.

Table 4.8 Technology, task and cognitive features of problems at each of the three main levels of proficiency

Level	Technology features	Task features	Cognitive processes
1	• Generic applications • Little or no navigation required • Relevant information is directly available • Use of facilitating tools not required	• Few steps • Single operators	• Reach a given goal • Apply explicit criteria • Minimal monitoring demands • Simple relevance match • Categorical reasoning • No integration or transformation
2	• Both generic and novel applications (e.g. web-based services) • Some navigation required to acquire information or perform actions • Use of tools facilitates operations	• Multiple steps • Multiple operators	• Goal may need to be defined • Apply explicit criteria • Generally higher monitoring demands • Generally involves resolving impasses • Some evaluation of relevance • Some integration or transformation • Inferential reasoning
3	• Generic and novel applications • Some navigation required to acquire information or perform actions • Use of tools required to efficiently solve the problem	• Multiple steps • Multiple operators	• Goal may need to be defined • Establish and apply criteria • Generally high monitoring • High inferential reasoning and integration • Evaluate relevance and reliability • Generally involves resolving impasses

Table 4.9 Proficiency levels: Problem solving in technology-rich environments

Level	Score range	The types of tasks completed successfully at each level of proficiency
Below Level 1	Below than 241 points	Tasks are based on well-defined problems involving the use of only one function within a generic interface to meet one explicit criterion without any categorical, inferential reasoning or transforming of information. Few steps are required and no sub goal has to be generated.
1	241 to less than 291 points	At this level, tasks typically require the use of widely available and familiar technology applications, such as e-mail software or a web browser. There is little or no navigation required to access the information or commands required to solve the problem. The problem may be solved regardless of the respondent's awareness and use of specific tools and functions (e.g. a sort function). The tasks involve few steps and a minimal number of operators. At the cognitive level, the respondent can readily infer the goal from the task statement; problem resolution requires the respondent to apply explicit criteria; and there are few monitoring demands (e.g. the respondent does not have to check whether he or she has used the appropriate procedure or made progress towards the solution). Identifying contents and operators can be done through simple match. Only simple forms of reasoning, such as assigning items to categories, are required; there is no need to contrast or integrate information.
2	291 to less than 341 points	At this level, tasks typically require the use of both generic and more specific technology applications. For instance, the respondent may have to make use of a novel online form. Some navigation across pages and applications is required to solve the problem. The use of tools (e.g. a sort function) can facilitate the resolution of the problem. The task may involve multiple steps and operators. The goal of the problem may have to be defined by the respondent, though the criteria to be met are explicit. There are higher monitoring demands. Some unexpected outcomes or impasses may appear. The task may require evaluating the relevance of a set of items to discard distractors. Some integration and inferential reasoning may be needed.
3	Equal to or higher than 341 points	At this level, tasks typically require the use of both generic and more specific technology applications. Some navigation across pages and applications is required to solve the problem. The use of tools (e.g. a sort function) is required to make progress towards the solution. The task may involve multiple steps and operators. The goal of the problem may have to be defined by the respondent, and the criteria to be met may or may not be explicit. There are typically high monitoring demands. Unexpected outcomes and impasses are likely to occur. The task may require evaluating the relevance and reliability of information in order to discard distractors. Integration and inferential reasoning may be needed to a large extent.

For instance, a problem is likely to be more complex if it involves the combined use of more than one computer application (e.g. e-mail and a spreadsheet); similarly, a problem is more complex if the task is defined in vague terms, as opposed to fully specified. Finally, a problem is likely to be more difficult if the respondent has to generate lots of deductions and inferences than if he or she just has to assemble or match different pieces of explicit information. The relationship between these dimensions and the proficiency levels is presented in Table 4.8. The descriptors of the levels are presented in Table 4.9.

Table 4.10 shows the probability of adults with particular proficiency in problem solving in technology-rich environments completing problem solving items of different levels of difficulty.

Table 4.10 Probability of successfully completing items at different difficulty levels by proficiency score: Problem solving in technology-rich environments

Item difficulty	Proficiency score									
	190	215	240	265	290	315	340	365	390	415
Level 1	0.02	0.06	0.17	0.40	0.69	0.87	0.95	0.98	0.99	1.00
Level 2	0.03	0.05	0.10	0.19	0.35	0.56	0.76	0.88	0.94	0.97
Level 3	0.00	0.01	0.02	0.05	0.13	0.29	0.49	0.67	0.80	0.87

A note about the reporting of problem solving in technology-rich environments

The populations for whom proficiency scores for problem solving in technology-rich environments are reported *are not identical* across countries/economies. Proficiency scores relate only to the proportion of the target population in each participating country that was able to undertake the computer-based version of the assessment, and thus meets the preconditions for displaying competency in this domain.

Four groups of respondents did not take the computer-based assessment,[2] those who:

- indicated in completing the background questionnaire that they had never used a computer (group 1)
- had some experience with computers but who "failed" the ICT core assessment (see Chapter 3) designed to determine whether a respondent had the basic computer skills necessary to undertake the computer-based assessment (group 2)
- had some experience with computers but opted not to take the computer-based assessment (group 3)
- did not attempt the ICT core for literacy-related reasons (group 4).

By definition, a minimum level of competency in the use of computer tools and applications and a minimum level of proficiency in literacy and numeracy is required in order to display proficiency in problem solving in technology-rich environments. Individuals in groups 1 and 2 are, thus, treated as not meeting the necessary preconditions for displaying proficiency and have no proficiency score in the domain of problem solving in technology-rich environments.

Respondents who did not attempt the ICT core for literacy-related reasons (group 4) have not been attributed a problem-solving score due to lack of sufficient information.

Respondents who opted not to take the computer-based assessment (group 3), however, represent a different category. They are individuals who, on their own initiative, decided to take the paper-and-pencil version of the assessment without going through the process designed to direct respondents to the computer-based or paper pathways of the assessment. As a result, it is not known whether or not they possessed the computer skills necessary to complete the computer-based assessment.

Three options for how to treat this group were considered: imputing their proficiency in problem solving on the basis of their proficiency in literacy and numeracy and their background characteristics; treating them as non-respondents; or reporting them as a separate category of the group that could not display competency. The latter option was adopted. Imputation was rejected on the grounds that refusals appeared to have different characteristics to respondents taking the computer-based assessment pathway. In fact, they appeared to be more similar to the respondents who did not have computer skills than to those who took the computer-based assessment. The option of treating them as non-respondents was rejected for similar reasons.

In reporting the results concerning problem solving in technology-rich environments, the following approach was adopted:

- When reporting proficiency in problem solving in technology-rich environments on the continuous scale at the country level, the proportion of the population displaying proficiency is reported in conjunction with country-level statistics (e.g. means, standard deviations, etc).

- When reporting distributions of the population by proficiency levels, information is presented for the entire adult population as a whole (i.e. those displaying proficiency plus those not displaying proficiency). The number or proportion of the population not displaying proficiency is always reported when results are presented by proficiency level.

TEST LANGUAGES AND REPORTING

In each participating country/economy, the Survey of Adult Skills was administered in the official national language(s) of the country and, in some cases, in a widely used language in addition to the national language(s). A small number of countries/economies administered the cognitive assessments in the national language only but administered the background questionnaire in the national language and a widely spoken language. The objective there was to minimise the number of respondents who failed to provide information for language-related reasons. Table 4.11 shows the languages in which the survey was administered.

Table 4.11 **Test languages by country**

OECD countries and economies	Language(s) of the cognitive assessment	Language(s) of the background questionnaire
Australia	English	English
Austria	German	German, Bosnian/Serbian/Croatian, Turkish
Canada	English, French	English, French
Chile	Spanish	Spanish
Czech Republic	Czech	Czech
Denmark	Danish	Danish
England (UK)	English	English
Estonia	Estonian, Russian	Estonian, Russian
Finland	Finnish, Swedish	Finnish, Swedish
Flanders (Belgium)	Dutch	Dutch
France	French	French
Germany	German	German
Greece	Greek	Greek
Ireland	English	English
Israel	Hebrew, Arabic, Russian	Hebrew, Arabic, Russian
Italy	Italian	Italian
Japan	Japanese	Japanese
Korea	Korean	Korean
Netherlands	Dutch	Dutch
New Zealand	English	English
Northern Ireland (UK)	English	English
Norway	Norwegian	Norwegian, English
Poland	Polish	Polish
Slovak Republic	Slovak, Hungarian	Slovak, Hungarian
Slovenia	Slovenian	Slovenian
Spain	Castilian, Catalan, Basque, Galician, Valencian	Castilian, Catalan, Basque, Galician, Valencian
Sweden	Swedish	Swedish
Turkey	Turkish	Turkish
United States	English	English, Spanish
Partners		
Cyprus[1]	Greek	Greek
Jakarta (Indonesia)	Indonesian	Indonesian
Lithuania	Lithuanian	Lithuanian
Russian Federation[2]	Russian	Russian
Singapore	English, Chinese	English

1. *Note by Turkey:* The information in this document with reference to "Cyprus" relates to the southern part of the Island. There is no single authority representing both Turkish and Greek Cypriot people on the Island. Turkey recognises the Turkish Republic of Northern Cyprus (TRNC). Until a lasting and equitable solution is found within the context of the United Nations, Turkey shall preserve its position concerning the "Cyprus issue".

Note by all the European Union Member States of the OECD and the European Union: The Republic of Cyprus is recognised by all members of the United Nations with the exception of Turkey. The information in this document relates to the area under the effective control of the Government of the Republic of Cyprus.

2. See note at the end of this chapter.
Countries and economies are ranked in alphabetical order.

For those countries/economies that tested in more than one language, results are presented as a single proficiency score. In other words, the mean proficiency score for literacy in Estonia, for example, is the mean proficiency of Estonian adults in reading in either Estonian or Russian. In only one country, Canada, was the sample designed to allow for reliable proficiency estimates in each of the languages in which the test was administered (in this case, English and French). However, as is the case for all other countries in which the test was administered in more than one language, Canadian results are presented in the international report in the form of a single proficiency estimate rather than as separate estimates for English and French speakers.

The Survey of Adult Skills was designed to assess the proficiency of the adult population in reading, in working with numbers, and in solving problems in the language(s) that are most relevant to and/or commonly used in the economic and civic life (e.g. in interaction with public bodies and institutions, in educational institutions) of a participating country. Therefore, poor performance in the test language(s) among non-native speakers of those languages, such as immigrants and their children, is not necessarily indicative of poor performance, as such. In the case of non-native speakers of the test language(s), low proficiency cannot be assumed to indicate low proficiency in their native language. A Turkish immigrant in Germany, for example, may display poor skills in the test language (German) but be a proficient reader and have good problem-solving skills when working in Turkish.

Notes

1. This differs from the approach used in IALS and ALL in which a value of 0.80 was used to locate items and test takers on the relevant scales. Further information on the change in approach and its impact is provided in Annex A.

2. Defined as taking, at a minimum, the core literacy and numeracy assessments on the computer.

A note regarding the Russian Federation

The sample for the Russian Federation does not include the population of the Moscow municipal area. The data published, therefore, do not represent the entire resident population aged 16-65 in the Russian Federation but rather the population of the Russian Federation *excluding* the population residing in the Moscow municipal area.

More detailed information regarding the data from the Russian Federation as well as that of other countries can be found in the *Technical Report of the Survey of Adult Skills, Second Edition* (OECD, forthcoming).

References

OECD (2012), *Literacy, Numeracy and Problem Solving in Technology-Rich Environments: Framework for the OECD Survey of Adult Skills,* OECD Publishing, Paris, http://dx.doi.org/10.1787/9789264128859-en.

PIAAC Expert Group in Problem Solving in Technology-Rich Environments (2009), "PIAAC Problem Solving in Technology-Rich Environments: A Conceptual Framework", OECD Education Working Papers, No. 36, OECD Publishing, Paris, http://dx.doi.org/10.1787/220262483674.

5

Relationship of the Survey of Adult Skills (PIAAC) to other international skills surveys

This chapter examines the relationship between the Survey of Adult Skills (PIAAC) and previous international skills surveys, notably the International Adult Literacy Survey (IALS) and the Adult Literacy and Life Skills Survey (ALL). It also discusses the differences and similarities between the Survey of Adult Skills and the Literacy Assessment and Monitoring Programme (LAMP) of UNESCO and the STEP Measurement Study, conducted by the World Bank.

Prior to the Survey of Adult Skills (PIAAC), two international assessments of adult skills were conducted in OECD countries: the International Adult Literacy Survey (IALS) of 1994-98 and the Adult Literacy and Life Skills Survey (ALL) of 2003-07.[1] In total, 18 countries/economies participating in the Survey of Adult Skills also participated in one or both of its predecessors. In addition, both UNESCO (the Literacy Assessment and Monitoring Programme – LAMP) and the World Bank (the STEP Measurement Study) have also conducted adult literacy and skills surveys in recent years.

This chapter describes the relationship between the Survey of Adult Skills and these other international adult skills surveys. Its objective is to help readers understand the links between the surveys and the factors that need to be taken into account when comparing results. It focuses on the Survey of Adult Skills, and IALS and ALL given the fact that many countries/economies participating in the Survey of Adult Skills also participated in IALS and/or ALL, and given the ultimate objective of providing comparable measures of proficiency in the domains of literacy and numeracy. Specifically, the discussion covers the factors that affect the degree to which valid comparisons may be made among the literacy and numeracy scores from the Survey of Adult Skills and the other assessments (see, for example, Mislevy, 1992), in particular:

- The comparability of the constructs measured and the content of the instruments used
- The comparability of the populations assessed
- The degree of similarity of the methodology used when conducting the survey.

The first four sections of the chapter cover the relationship between the Survey of Adult Skills and IALS and ALL, including information on the countries/economies for which repeated measures of literacy and/or numeracy proficiency are available; links between the surveys, in terms of the constructs, assessment instruments and background questionnaires; and the operational aspects of the three surveys. The final section describes the relationship between the Survey of Adult Skills and LAMP and STEP, respectively.

COUNTRIES AND ECONOMIES PARTICIPATING IN THE SURVEY OF ADULT SKILLS (PIAAC) AND IALS AND/OR ALL

In total, 18 of the countries or economies participating in the first two rounds of the Survey of Adult Skills participated in IALS, and six participated in both IALS and ALL (Table 5.1). IALS was undertaken in three separate waves with data collection occurring in 1994, 1996 and 1998. ALL was undertaken in two waves with data collection taking place in 2003 and 2006-07. Table 5.1 lists the countries/economies participating in each of IALS, ALL and PIAAC together with the dates of data collection.

Table 5.1 **Countries and economies participating in IALS, ALL and PIAAC: Dates of data collection**

OECD countries and economies	IALS	ALL	PIAAC
Australia	1996	2006	2011/12
Canada	1994	2003	2011/12
Chile	1998	-	2014/15
Czech Republic	1998	-	2011/12
Denmark	1998	-	2011/12
England (UK)	1996	-	2011/12
Finland	1998	-	2011/12
Flanders (Belgium)	1996	-	2011/12
Germany	1994	-	2011/12
Ireland	1996	-	2011/12
Italy	1998	2003	2011/12
Netherlands	1994	2006	2011/12
New Zealand	1996	2007	2011/12
Northern Ireland (UK)	1996	-	2011/12
Norway	1998	2003	2011/12
Poland	1994	-	2011/12
Slovenia	1998	-	2014/15
Sweden	1994	-	2011/12
United States	1994	2003	2011/12

Countries and economies are ranked in alphabetical order.

CONSTRUCTS AND INSTRUMENTS: THE SURVEY OF ADULT SKILLS, ALL AND IALS

The domains of skills assessed in the Survey of Adult Skills and its predecessors are presented graphically in Table 5.2. Shading indicates links between assessments in terms of the constructs measured and the content of the assessment instruments.

The domains of literacy, including reading components, and problem solving in technology-rich environments, as assessed in the Survey of Adult Skills, represent new domains of assessment, notwithstanding the close links between literacy as conceived and measured in the Survey of Adult Skills and prose and document literacy as assessed in IALS and ALL. Reading components is also a new domain. The conceptualisation of numeracy in the Survey of Adult Skills is very close to that used in ALL.

Table 5.2 Skills assessed in the Survey of Adult Skills (PIAAC), ALL and IALS

Survey of Adult Skills (PIAAC) (2012)	ALL (2003-2007)	IALS (1994-1998)
Literacy (encompasses the reading of prose and document texts as well as digital texts)	Literacy (rescaled to combine prose and document literacy)	Literacy (rescaled to combine prose and document literacy)
	Prose literacy	Prose literacy
	Document literacy	Document literacy
Reading components		
Numeracy	Numeracy	
		Quantitative literacy
Problem solving in technology-rich environments		
	Problem solving	

Note: The same colour indicates comparability between surveys in the domains concerned.

Literacy

As defined in the Survey of Adult Skills, literacy is conceived more broadly than in IALS and ALL. Literacy encompasses the domains of prose and document literacy,[2] which were assessed separately in IALS and ALL. In addition, literacy includes the reading of digital texts in addition to the reading of print-based texts (see Chapter 1). Apart from including digital texts and mixed-format texts (i.e. texts containing both continuous and non-continuous elements) in the corpus of texts defining the domain, there is, by design, considerable overlap between the concept of literacy and those of prose and document literacy (see OECD/Statistics Canada, 2005, pp. 277-290, for a description of the conceptualisation of prose and document literacy). The conceptualisation of the cognitive processes used in gaining meaning from text, the definition of the contexts in which reading takes place and the factors affecting the difficulty of test items are very similar.

In addition, the Survey of Adult Skills is linked to IALS and ALL through the use of a number of common test items. Twenty-nine of the 52 literacy items included in the computer-based version of the literacy assessment were linking items (i.e. items that had been used in the assessments of prose and document literacy in IALS and/or ALL). In the paper-based versions, 18 of the 24 items administered were linking items. Reading components represents a new element of the assessment of literacy that was not included in either IALS or ALL.

The reading-components assessment in the Survey of Adult Skills should not be confused with the identically named reading-components assessment of the International Study of Reading Skills (ISRS) (Grenier et al., 2008), administered in 2005 to a sample of respondents to ALL in Canada and to a sample of just over 1 000 adults (for the most part enrolled in adult literacy centres) in the United States (Strucker, Kirsch and Yamamoto, 2007). The ISRS tested word recognition, vocabulary, basic text processing and spelling.[3] The only direct point of convergence between the ISRS and the Survey of Adult Skills is in the area of vocabulary, where a broadly similar approach was used.

Numeracy

The conceptualisation of numeracy in the Survey of Adult Skills is similar to that used in ALL. As can be seen in Table 5.2 above, the domain of numeracy was introduced in ALL to replace that of quantitative literacy, which had been measured in IALS. Quantitative literacy covered the skills needed to undertake arithmetic operations such as addition, subtraction, multiplication, and division, either singly or in combination, using numbers or quantities embedded in printed material.

Numeracy is conceived as a broader domain than quantitative literacy, covering a wider range of quantitative skills and knowledge, not just computational operations. It also covers a broader range of situations in which actors have to deal with mathematical information of different types, not just situations involving numbers embedded in printed materials (Gal et al., 2005, p. 151). As in the case of the literacy assessment, a number of numeracy items are common to both the Survey of Adult Skills and ALL. Of the 52 literacy items included in the computer-based version of the numeracy assessment, 30 were taken from ALL. In the paper-based versions, 19 of the 24 items administered had been previously used in ALL.

Problem solving in technology-rich environments

The domain of problem solving in technology-rich environments is one that has not previously been assessed. In particular, its emphasis on "information problems" and the solution of problems in an ICT context, rather than on analytic problem-solving skills per se, distinguishes it from previous conceptualisations of problem solving.[4]

Mode of delivery

A major difference between the Survey of Adult Skills and IALS and ALL is that it was designed as a computer-based assessment (with a pencil-and-paper option for respondents who did not have sufficient computer skills to take the assessment in computer-based mode). In contrast, both IALS and ALL were exclusively paper-and-pencil-based assessments in which respondents received printed booklets in which they responded to questions in writing.

Despite the similarity in the skills measured and the use of common items, the difference in the delivery mode adopted for the Survey of Adult Skills compared to IALS and ALL had the potential to negatively affect the comparability of results in the domains of literacy and numeracy. It was possible that response patterns could be affected by the mode of delivery of test items; and the difficulty and degree of discrimination of some items could vary according to whether they were answered in computer-based or paper-based format.

The existence and extent of mode effects was explored in the field test, which was implemented from March to July 2010. A proportion of respondents undertaking the field test in each country was randomly assigned to either the computer-based or paper-based version of the assessment.[5] The results for the two randomly equivalent samples were compared. Overall, no significant mode effects were identified.[6]

COMPARABILITY OF BACKGROUND QUESTIONS

The extent to which comparisons can be made between the Survey of Adult Skills and its predecessors depends not only on the psychometric links between the assessments. For the results for subgroups of the population to be reliably compared between surveys, the definitions of the relevant subgroups must be similar between the surveys.

In areas such as the personal characteristics of respondents, language background, immigration status, educational attainment and participation, and labour-force status, there is high degree of similarity between the questions and response categories used in the Survey of Adult Skills and those used in IALS and ALL. Comparable information is also collected regarding literacy, numeracy and ICT use at work. Where there are differences in response categories, derived variables were created to facilitate comparisons between assessments; these have been included in published data files with full documentation for analysts. Annex B provides a list of the background variables common to the Survey of Adult Skills and one or both of IALS and ALL.

A revised version of the International Standard Classification of Occupations (ISCO) – ISCO-08 – was adopted in 2007, replacing the former ISCO-88 (ILO, 2007). This has necessitated the mapping of the ISCO-88 categories used in the coding of occupations in IALS and ALL to the ISCO-08. As a consequence, comparisons can only be made at the one digit level between the occupational information contained in the Survey of Adult Skills and that available from IALS and ALL.

SURVEY METHODS AND OPERATIONAL STANDARDS AND PROCEDURES

Other things being equal, differences in design, methodology and operational procedures may have a potentially significant effect on the comparability of different assessments. This section presents a comparison of the extent of comparability between IALS, ALL and the Survey of Adult Skills in terms of:

- the target population
- sample design and procedures
- survey operations
- response rates.

The target population

The target population defined for both IALS and ALL is identical to that of the Survey of Adult Skills, i.e. civilian, non-institutionalised persons aged 16-65. In each of the three surveys, participating countries/economies were required to use sampling frames that covered the target population. Exclusions of up to a maximum of 5% of the target population were permitted.[7] The estimated coverage of the target population in each of the three surveys is presented in Table 5.3.

Table 5.3 **Population coverage: IALS, ALL and the Survey of Adult Skills (PIAAC)**

OECD countries and economies	IALS	ALL	PIAAC
Australia	98	>95	97
Canada	98	>95	98
Chile			100
Czech Republic	98		98
Denmark	99		95
England (UK)	97		98
Finland	94		97
Flanders (Belgium)	99		95
Germany	na		97
Ireland	100		100
Italy	na	>95	99
Netherlands	99	>95	97
New Zealand			98
Northern Ireland (UK)	97		98
Norway	99	>95	99
Poland	99		95
Slovenia			95
Sweden	98		99
United States	97	>95	99

Countries and economies are ranked in alphabetical order.
Source: OECD and Statistics Canada (2000), OECD, Statistics Canada (2011).

Sample design

In the Survey of Adult Skills, ALL and IALS, participating countries/economies were required to use a probability sample representative of the target population. Of the countries/economies participating in the Survey of Adult Skills and one or both of IALS or ALL, there is only one documented case of deviation from this requirement. In IALS, Germany employed a non-probability selection method at the second stage of its three-stage sample design (Murray et al., 1998, p. 28). However, the extent of deviation from strict probability sampling was assessed to be "relatively minor" and was not believed to have "introduced significant bias into the survey estimates" (Murray et al., 1998, p. 39).

Survey operations

Both the degree of standardisation of survey procedures and the effort put into monitoring compliance with these standards have been greater in the Survey of Adult Skills than was the case in either IALS or ALL. An external review of the implementation of the first round of IALS[8] conducted in the second half of 1995 (Kalton, Lyberg and Rempp, 1998) concluded that while there were no concerns regarding the development of instrumentation: "The variation in survey execution across countries is so large that we recommend that all comparative analyses across countries should be interpreted with due caution" (Kalton, Lyberg and Rempp, 1998, p. 4). In particular, while guidance on survey procedures was provided to the participating countries, the reviewers found that little was done to "enforce adherence to specific procedures" (Kalton, Lyberg and Rempp, 1998, p. 4). Quality-assurance procedures were subsequently improved for the second and third rounds of IALS (OECD/Statistics Canada, 2000, p. 129) and in ALL.[9]

Maximising standardisation in processes and procedures and, therefore, minimising any differentials in error resulting from variation in implementation was a central objective of the Survey of Adult Skills. The quality-assurance and quality control procedures put in place are among the most comprehensive and stringent ever implemented for an international household-based survey. The standards that participating countries/economies are required to meet in implementing the Survey of Adult Skills were set out in a comprehensive set of Technical Standards and Guidelines (PIAAC, 2014). These were accompanied by a quality-assurance and quality-control process that involved review of and sign-off by the international consortium at key stages of implementation (e.g. sampling designs) and data collection throughout the project. The results of the quality-control activity fed into an assessment of the overall quality of the data from each participating country.

Survey response

Non-response is a potentially significant source of error in any sample survey. In comparing results across the Survey of Adult Skills, IALS and ALL, it is important to be aware of the response rates for the different surveys. Table 5.4 presents the response rates of the three surveys for those countries/economies for which repeated observations are available.

Table 5.4 **Response rates: IALS, ALL and the Survey of Adult Skills (PIAAC)**

OECD countries and economies	IALS	ALL	PIAAC
Australia	96	79	71
Canada	69	66	59
Chile	74		66
Czech Republic	61		66
Denmark	66		50
England (UK)	63		59
Finland	69		66
Flanders (Belgium)	36		62
Germany	69		55
Ireland	60		72
Italy	35	44	56
Netherlands	45	47	51
New Zealand	74	64	63
Northern Ireland (UK)	58		65
Norway	61	56	62
Poland	75		56
Slovenia	70		62
Sweden	60		45
United States	60	66	70

Countries and economies are ranked in alphabetical order.
Source: OECD and Statistics Canada (2000), OECD, Statistics Canada (2011).

EDUCATIONAL ATTAINMENT IN IALS

For four countries participating in IALS (the Czech Republic, Germany, Poland and the United Kingdom), the proportion of the adult population classified as having educational attainment at lower secondary level (ISCED 0-2)[10] is considerably lower and the proportion with secondary attainment (ISCED 3-4) is considerably higher than is found in other statistics on educational attainment for the years as IALS data was collected (1994 or 1996 depending on the country) such as those published by the OECD in *Education at a Glance* (Gesthuizen, Solga and Künster, 2009). Analysts should bear this in mind when comparing results between IALS and ALL and the Survey of Adult Skills for these countries. Gesthuizen, Solga and Künster (2009) propose a method to correct the attribution of respondents to levels of educational attainment in the IALS data set that provides distributions in line with other attainment statistics.

SUMMARY OF THE RELATIONSHIP BETWEEN THE SURVEY OF ADULT SKILLS (PIAAC), IALS AND ALL

In summary, the Survey of Adult Skills was designed to be linked psychometrically with IALS and ALL in the domain of literacy and ALL in the domain of numeracy. Analysis of data from the field trial and from the main data collection confirmed that results from IALS, ALL and the Survey of Adult Skills could be placed on the same scale in literacy and that the results from the Survey of Adult Skills and ALL could be placed on the same scale in numeracy. At the same time, caution is advised in comparing the results of the Survey of Adult Skills and previous surveys, particularly IALS, due to possible variations in operational procedures and low response rates in some countries/economies.

THE RELATIONSHIP BETWEEN THE SURVEY OF ADULT SKILLS (PIAAC), LAMP AND STEP

Two other international surveys of adults that have been administered since 2003 – UNESCO's Literacy Assessment Monitoring Programme (LAMP) and the World Bank's STEP measurement study[11] – have assessed either the same (STEP) or related (LAMP) skills as the Survey of Adult Skills. Table 5.5 provides an overview of the common skills assessed in the three studies; the relationship of these studies to the Survey of Adult Skills is addressed in more detail below.

LAMP

The development of LAMP began in 2003 under the aegis of the UNESCO Institute for Statistics (UIS). Its aim is "to provide policymakers with robust information on population profiles in terms of literacy and numeracy" (UNESCO Institute for Statistics, 2009, p. 7). LAMP assesses proficiency in the domains of prose literacy, document literacy and numeracy. In addition, it involves an assessment of reading components (recognition of letters and numbers, word recognition, print vocabulary, sentence processing and passage fluency). The design of LAMP owes much to that of IALS and ALL. In particular, the conceptualisation of prose and document literacy and numeracy was based on the assessment frameworks developed for these studies. In each of the domains assessed, some items from IALS and ALL were included in the test instruments. Four countries and economies[12] have completed the assessment. The implementation of LAMP followed a rather different model from that adopted in the Survey of Adult Skills. In particular, the timing of implementation was left to the discretion of participating countries, and process of quality assurance and control was far lighter.

Table 5.5 **Skills assessed in the Survey of Adult Skills (PIAAC), STEP, LAMP, ALL and IALS**

Survey of Adult Skills (PIAAC)	STEP	LAMP	ALL	IALS
Literacy (combined prose and document and digital reading)	Literacy (combined prose and document)		Literacy (combined prose and document[1])	Literacy (combined prose and document[1])
		Prose literacy	Prose literacy	Prose literacy
		Document literacy	Document literacy	Document literacy
Reading components	Reading components	Reading components		
Numeracy		Numeracy	Numeracy	
				Quantitative literacy

Note: The same colour indicates comparability between surveys in the domains concerned.
1. Rescaled on the single Survey of Adult Skills (PIAAC) literacy scale.

Despite its relationship to IALS and ALL (and, by virtue of this, to the Survey of Adult Skills) at the level of the assessment frameworks, LAMP was not designed to have psychometric links to either of these surveys in any of the domains measured. In the presentation of results, the distinct nature of the LAMP scales was emphasised by using scales with values from 0-2 000 with a mean of 1 000 (as opposed to a 0-500 point scale) and by defining three (as opposed to five) proficiency levels.

STEP

The World Bank's STEP measurement study was launched in 2010 with the aim of enhancing the information available to policy makers regarding the level and distribution of skills relevant to the labour market in the adult populations of developing countries. Eight countries were involved in the first wave of data collection, which took place in 2011: Plurinational State of Bolivia, Colombia, Ghana, Laos People's Democratic Republic, Sri Lanka, Ukraine, Viet Nam, and Yunnan province of the People's Republic of China (hereafter "China"). The second wave, which took place in 2012/13, involved five countries, including: Armenia, Azerbaijan, Former Yugoslav Republic of Macedonia (FYROM), Georgia and Kenya.

The study contained a survey administered to individuals and an employer survey. The individual survey contained three modules focused on cognitive skills, technical skills and socio-emotional skills. In addition to collecting self-reported information regarding certain cognitive skills, the cognitive module involved administering a direct assessment of reading literacy based on the Survey of Adult Skills instruments.

The STEP literacy assessment involved two versions. The first used an extended version of the paper-based literacy assessment administered by the Survey of Adult Skills as well as the latter's reading components assessment. This was implemented in Armenia, Plurinational State of Bolivia, Colombia, Georgia, Ghana, Kenya, Ukraine and Viet Nam. The second used the literacy core test from the Survey of Adult Skills only, and was implemented in Former Yugoslav Republic of Macedonia (FYROM), Lao People's Democratic Republic, Sri Lanka and Yunnan province in China. The STEP literacy assessment was designed with the objective of recording results on the literacy scale of the Survey of Adult Skills.

There are important differences between STEP and the Survey of Adult Skills. First, the target population for STEP was not the resident adult population of the participating country or region as a whole but the population of urban centres. Second, although similar technical standards for the literacy assessment were followed in both surveys, the operational standards applied (including the quality-assurance and control processes) followed protocols established by each data collection agency. Both these factors need to be taken into account when comparing results from STEP and the Survey of Adult Skills.

Notes

1. See OECD/Statistics Canada (2000), OECD/Statistics Canada (2005) and OECD/Statistics Canada (2011) for information on the methods and results of IALS and ALL.

2. In IALS and ALL, prose literacy was defined as the knowledge and skills needed to understand and use continuous texts – information organised in sentence and paragraph formats. Document literacy represented the knowledge and skills needed to process documents (or non-continuous texts) in which information is organised in matrix structures (i.e. in rows and columns). The type of documents covered by this domain included tables, signs, indexes, lists, coupons, schedules, charts, graphs, maps, and forms.

3. Word recognition was assessed with the Test of Word Recognition Efficiency (TOWRE) – real words (TOWRE-A) and pseudo-words (TOWRE-B). Vocabulary was assessed with the abridged Peabody Picture Vocabulary Test (PPVT-m), general processing skills were assessed with the Rapid Automatized Naming (RAN) test and the Digit-Span test, and spelling with an abridged version of a test developed by Moats (Grenier, et al., 2008, p. 94).

4. In ALL, problem solving was defined as "goal-directed thinking and action in situations for which no routine solution procedure is available" (OECD/Statistics Canada, 2005, p.16).

5. Of the respondents who passed the ICT core, 27% were directed to the paper-based assessment and 63% to the computer-based assessment.

6. A complete description of the field test design and analysis of mode effects can be found in Chapters 18 and 19 of the *Technical Report of the Survey of Adult Skills, Second Edition* (OECD, forthcoming).

7. Exclusions were permitted for "practical operational" reasons in ALL (OECD/Statistics Canada, 2005, p. 216). Murray, Kirsch and Jenkins (1998, p. 26) provides a list of exclusions in participating countries for the first wave of IALS.

8. The first round involved nine countries: Canada, France, Germany, Ireland, the Netherlands, Poland, Sweden, Switzerland, and the United States. France withdrew from the study in 1995 citing concerns regarding data quality.

9. A technical report covering the first wave of IALS was published in 1998 (Murray, Kirsch and Jenkins [eds], 1998). Some information on the implementation of the 2nd and 3rd rounds of IALS and the implementation of ALL is available in the methodological appendices of OECD/Statistics Canada (2000), OECD/Statistics Canada (2005), and OECD/Statistics Canada (2011). However, technical reports covering the 2nd and 3rd rounds of IALS and the two rounds of ALL have not been released.

10. ISCED is the International Standard Classification of Education.

11. Information regarding LAMP can be found at: www.uis.unesco.org/literacy/Pages/lamp-literacy-assessment.aspx and information regarding STEP in Gaëlle et al. (2014).

12. Jordan, Mongolia, Palestinian Authority and Paraguay.

References

Gal, I., M. van Groenestijn, M. Manly, M.J. Schmitt and **D. Tout** (2005), "Adult Numeracy and its Assessment in the ALL Survey: A Conceptual Framework and Pilot Results", in S. Murray, Y. Clermont and M. Binkley (eds) (2005), *Measuring Adult Literacy and Life Skills: New frameworks for Assessment*, Statistics Canada, Ottawa, Catalogue No. 89-552-MIE, No. 13.

Gaëlle, P., M.L. Sanchez Puerta, A. Valerio and **T. Rajadel** (2014), "STEP Skills Measurement Surveys - Innovative Tools for Assessing Skills", *Social Protection & Labor Discussion Paper 1421*, World Bank Group.

Gesthuizen, M., H. Solga and **R. Künster** (2009), "Context Matters: Economic Marginalization of Low-educated Workers in Crossnational Perspective", in *European Sociological Review*, Vol. 27, No. 2, 2011, pp. 264-280.

Grenier, S., S. Jones, J. Strucker, T.S. Murray, G. Gervais and **S. Brink** (2008), *Learning Literacy in Canada: Evidence from the International Survey of Reading Skills*, Statistics Canada, Ottawa, Catalogue No. 89-552-MIE, No. 19.

International Labour Organization (ILO) (2007), "Resolution Concerning Updating the International Standard Classification of Occupations", www.ilo.org/public/english/bureau/stat/isco/docs/resol08.pdf.

Kalton, G., L. Lyberg and **J.-M. Rempp** (1998), "Review of Methodology", in T.S. Murray, I. Kirsch and L. Jenkins (eds) (1988), *Adult Literacy in OECD Countries: Technical Report on the First International Adult Literacy Survey*, National Center for Education Statistics, Office of Educational Research and Improvement, Washington, DC.

Mislevy, R.J. (1992), *Linking Educational Assessments: Concepts, Issues, Methods, and Prospects*, Policy Information Center, Educational Testing Service, Princeton.

Murray, T.S., I. Kirsch and **L. Jenkins** (eds) (1998), *Adult Literacy in OECD Countries: Technical Report on the First International Adult Literacy Survey*, National Center for Education Statistics, Office of Educational Research and Improvement, Washington, DC.

OECD (forthcoming), *Technical Report of the Survey of Adult Skills, Second Edition*.

OECD/Statistics Canada (2011), *Literacy for Life: Further Results from the Adult Literacy and Life Skills Survey*, OECD Publishing, Paris, http://dx.doi.org/10.1787/9789264091269-en.

OECD/Statistics Canada (2005), *Learning a Living: First Results of the Adult Literacy and Life Skills Survey*, OECD Publishing, Paris, http://dx.doi.org/10.1787/9789264010390-en.

OECD/Statistics Canada (2000), *Literacy in the Information Age: Final Report of the International Adult Literacy Survey*, OECD Publishing, Paris, http://dx.doi.org/10.1787/9789264181762-en.

PIAAC (2014), *PIAAC Technical Standards and Guidelines*, OECD Programme for the International Assessment of Adult Competencies, www.oecd.org/site/piaac/PIAAC-NPM%282014_06%29PIAAC_Technical_Standards_and_Guidelines.pdf.

Strucker, J., I. Kirsch and **K. Yamamoto** (2007), *The Relationship of the Component Skills of Reading to IALS Performance: Tipping Points and Five Classes of Adult Literacy Learners*, NCSALL Reports #29, National Center for the Study of Adult Learning and Literacy, Cambridge, www.ncsall.net/fileadmin/resources/research/report_29_ials.pdf.

UNESCO Institute for Statistics (UIS) (2009), *The Next Generation of Literacy Statistics: Implementing the Literacy Assessment and Monitoring Programme (LAMP)*, Technical Paper No. 1, UNESCO Institute for Statistics, Montreal, www.uis.unesco.org/Library/Documents/Tech1-eng.pdf.

World Bank (n.d.), *STEP Skills Measurement Study,* http://siteresources.worldbank.org/EXTHDOFFICE/Resources/5485726-1281723119684/STEP_Skills_Measurement_Brochure_Jan_2012.pdf.

6

Relationship between the Survey of Adult Skills (PIAAC) and the OECD Programme for International Student Assessment (PISA)

This chapter explains how the Survey of Adult Skills (PIAAC) and the OECD Programme for International Student Assessment (PISA) are related. Although there are similarities between the two in how skills are defined, there are significant differences between the two assessments, including the target populations and the measures used to assess skills.

6

RELATIONSHIP BETWEEN THE SURVEY OF ADULT SKILLS (PIAAC) AND THE OECD PROGRAMME FOR INTERNATIONAL STUDENT ASSESSMENT (PISA)

In most of the countries/economies participating in the Survey of Adult Skills (PIAAC), respondents aged 16-30 will be members of cohorts that have taken part in the OECD Programme for International Student Assessment (PISA). In addition, both PISA and the Survey of Adult Skills assess ostensibly similar skills – in particular, literacy and numeracy, but also problem solving. Given the overlap in terms of the cohorts assessed and the content of the assessments, it is important that users understand the similarities and differences between the two studies and the extent to which results of the two studies can be compared.

This chapter provides an overview of the relationship between the Survey of Adult Skills and PISA and emphasises two key points. First, the Survey of Adult Skills was not designed to be linked psychometrically to PISA. Even in those areas in which there are the greatest links conceptually (in the domains of literacy/reading literacy and numeracy/mathematical literacy), the measurement scales are distinct. Second, the conceptualisation of the skills of literacy and numeracy in the Survey of Adult Skills has much in common with that of the skills of reading literacy and mathematical literacy in PISA.

PISA COHORTS IN THE TARGET POPULATION OF THE SURVEY OF ADULT SKILLS (PIAAC)

The target population for the Survey of Adult Skills includes the cohorts that participated in PISA 2000, 2003, 2006, 2009 and 2012. The age of the cohorts assessed in the four rounds of PISA between 2000 and 2012 at the time of the data collection for Rounds 1 and 2 of the Survey of Adult Skills is presented in Table 6.1.

Table 6.1 **Age of PISA cohorts in 2011-12 and 2014-15**

	Age in 2011-12	Age in 2014-15
PISA 2000	26-27	29-30
PISA 2003	23-24	26-27
PISA 2006	20-21	23-24
PISA 2009	17-18	20-21
PISA 2012		17-18

DIFFERENCES IN THE TARGET POPULATIONS

As noted above, several "PISA cohorts" are included in the population assessed in the Survey of Adult Skills. There are differences in coverage of these cohorts in PISA and the adult survey which need to be taken into account in any comparison of the results from the two assessments. In particular, the target population of the Survey of Adult Skills is broader than that of PISA and the PISA cohorts assessed by it include individuals who were not part of the PISA target population.

The target population of PISA is young people aged between 15 years and 3 months and 16 years and 2 months at the beginning of the assessment period who were *enrolled in an educational institution at Grade 7 or above* (OECD, 2010a). Fifteen-year-olds who are not enrolled at an educational institution are not tested as part of PISA and, in all countries participating in the four rounds of PISA between 2000 and 2009, a proportion of 15-year-olds were out of school or in grades lower than Grade 7. In 2009, for example, the PISA sample represented between 94% (Belgium) and 82% (United States) of the 15-year-old population in the countries covered in this report (OECD, 2010a, Table A2.1). The target population for the Survey of Adult Skills is the entire *resident* population. Therefore, the "PISA cohorts" surveyed in the Survey of Adult Skills include, in addition to persons who were at school at age 15 (and, therefore, part of the PISA target population), those who were out of school at the age of 15 (and, therefore, outside the PISA target population). Irrespective of any other considerations, the different rates of coverage of the cohorts are relevant to comparisons of the results of the two surveys for the "PISA cohorts". In particular, it seems likely that, in most countries, mean proficiency scores for the full 15-year-old cohort would have been lower than those observed for 15-year-olds who were in school,[1] as the available evidence suggests that early school-leavers are less proficient than students who continue in schooling (see, for example, Bushnik, Barr-Telford and Bussière, 2003 and Fullarton et al., 2003).

SKILLS ASSESSED

Table 6.2 shows the skill domains assessed in the Survey of Adult Skills and those assessed in the four rounds of PISA that have been administered since 2000. As can be seen, both studies assess skills in the domains of literacy, numeracy/ mathematics and problem solving. The one area in which there is no overlap is that of scientific literacy.

6

RELATIONSHIP BETWEEN THE SURVEY OF ADULT SKILLS (PIAAC) AND THE OECD PROGRAMME FOR INTERNATIONAL STUDENT ASSESSMENT (PISA)

Table 6.2 **Comparison of the Survey of Adult Skills (PIAAC) and PISA: Skills assessed**

The Survey of Adult Skills (PIAAC)	PISA
Literacy	Reading literacy (2000, 2003, 2006, 2009, 2012)
	Electronic reading (2009)
Numeracy	Mathematical literacy (2000, 2003, 2006, 2009, 2012)
Problem solving in technology-rich environments	Problem solving (2003), (2012)
	Scientific literacy (2000, 2003, 2006, 2009, 2012)

PSYCHOMETRIC LINKS

The Survey of Adult Skills was not designed to allow direct comparisons of its results with those of PISA. Despite similarities in the broad approach to defining the skills assessed, the two surveys include no common items, and the results from the two surveys cannot be treated as being on the same scale in any of the domains that they ostensibly have in common.

An objective of the first round of PISA was to establish a psychometric link between PISA and the International Adult Literacy Survey (IALS) in the domain of literacy (see OECD, 1999, p. 29). Fifteen prose items from IALS were embedded in the PISA 2000 test booklets for the main study. Items from IALS were not included in the assessments of reading literacy conducted in subsequent rounds of PISA, however.

The outcomes of an analysis investigating whether students taking the PISA 2000 assessment could be placed on the IALS prose literacy scale is reported in Yamamoto (2002) and *Reading for Change: Performance and Engagement across Countries: Results from PISA 2000* (OECD, 2002). Yamamoto concluded that PISA students could be placed on the IALS prose literacy scale.[2] Chapter 8 of *Reading for Change* (OECD, 2002) presents the distribution of students in participating countries across the five IALS proficiency levels.

THE RELATIONSHIPS BETWEEN CONSTRUCTS IN THE DOMAINS OF LITERACY, NUMERACY AND PROBLEM SOLVING

While there has been no attempt to link the Survey of Adult Skills to PISA in any assessment domains, the two studies share a similar approach to assessment, both in terms of broad orientation and the definition of the domains assessed.

Both the Survey of Adult Skills and PISA hold an action-oriented or functional conception of skills. The object of interest is the application and use of knowledge and know-how in common life situations as opposed to the mastery of a body of knowledge or of a repertoire of techniques. In defining assessment domains, the emphasis is placed on the purposive and reflective use and processing of information to achieve a variety of goals. To this end, in both studies, the skills assessed are defined in terms of a set of behaviours through which the skill is manifested and a set of goals that the behaviours in question are intended to achieve.

The Survey of Adult Skills and PISA also share a common approach to the specification of the constructs measured.[3] The frameworks defining the constructs specify their features in terms of three dimensions: content, cognitive processes and context. The dimension of *content* ("knowledge domain" in PISA) relates to the artefacts, tools, knowledge, representations, cognitive challenges, etc. that constitute the corpus to which an individual (an adult, in the case of the Survey of Adult Skills; a 15-year-old student in the case of PISA) must respond or that he or she must use. *Cognitive strategies* ("competencies" in PISA) cover the mental processes that individuals bring into play to respond to or use given content in an appropriate manner. *Context* ("context and situation" in PISA) refers to the different situations in which individuals read, display numerate behaviour, solve problems or use scientific knowledge.

The similarities and differences between the conceptualisation of the domains of literacy, numeracy and problem solving in the Survey of Adult Skills and those of reading literacy, mathematical literacy and problem solving in PISA are discussed below through a comparison of the respective assessment frameworks.[4]

Literacy

Table 6.3 provides a summary of the definition and the content, processes and context dimensions of the literacy framework of the Survey of Adult Skills and the reading literacy framework for PISA.

6

RELATIONSHIP BETWEEN THE SURVEY OF ADULT SKILLS (PIAAC) AND THE OECD PROGRAMME FOR INTERNATIONAL STUDENT ASSESSMENT (PISA)

Table 6.3 **Comparison of the Survey of Adult Skills (PIAAC) and PISA: Literacy**

	Survey of Adult Skills (PIAAC)	**PISA**
Definition	The ability to understand, evaluate, use and engage with *written texts* to participate in society, to achieve one's goals, and to develop one's knowledge and potential.	The capacity to understand, use, reflect on and engage with written texts, in order to achieve one's goals, to develop one's knowledge and potential, and to participate in society.
Content	Different types of text. Texts are characterised by their medium (*print-based* or *digital*) and by their format: ▪ *Continuous* or *prose texts*, which involve narration, argumentation or descriptions, for example ▪ *Non-continuous* or *document texts*, for example, tables, lists and graphs ▪ *Mixed texts*, which involve combinations of prose and document elements ▪ *Multiple texts*, which consist of the juxtaposition or linking of independently generated elements	The form of reading materials: ▪ Continuous texts, including different kinds of prose such as narration, exposition, argumentation ▪ Non-continuous texts, including graphs, forms and lists ▪ Digital and print (from 2009)
Cognitive processes	Access and identify Integrate and interpret (relating parts of text to one another) Evaluate and reflect	Retrieving information Interpreting texts Reflecting on and evaluating texts
Contexts	Personal Work Community Education	Personal (e.g. a personal letter) Occupational (e.g. a report) Public (e.g. an official document) Educational (e.g. school-related reading)

Content

The Survey of Adult Skills and PISA (2000-12) share a common conceptualisation of the texts forming the corpus of written materials to which test-takers respond. Text formats are categorised as continuous (prose), non-continuous (document), mixed and multiple texts. In terms of their type or rhetorical character, there is considerable overlap in the categorisations used. Both frameworks identify description, narration, exposition, argumentation and instructions. The framework for the Survey of Adult Skills also includes the additional category of "records" (the documentation of decisions and events) and the PISA framework (OECD, 2010b, p. 33) identifies the text type, "transaction" (a text that aims to achieve a specific purpose outlined in the text, such as requesting that something is done, organising a meeting or making a social engagement with a friend). There is some variation in the distribution of the texts used in the actual assessments by format. Mixed texts are the most frequent text format found in the Survey of Adult Skills whereas continuous texts are the format most frequently found in PISA.[5]

Cognitive processes

PISA 2000 identified five types of cognitive process required to understand and respond to texts that were grouped into three broader categories ("access and retrieve", "integrate and interpret" and "evaluate and reflect") for the purpose of analysis. By PISA 2009 only the three broader categories were retained. The framework for the Survey of Adult Skills uses the same three categories to organise the cognitive operations used in reading. In the actual assessments, the Survey of Adult Skills includes a greater share of access and retrieve tasks than does PISA, while PISA includes a greater proportion of items requiring evaluation and reflection. This reflects the different expert groups' judgements as to relative importance of the different types of tasks performed by 15-year-olds and adults in their ordinary reading.

Contexts

Reading is a purposeful activity that takes place in a context. While the actual contexts cannot be simulated in an assessment, the frameworks of both assessments seek to ensure that a reasonable coverage of such contexts is represented in the respective assessments. While using slightly different wording, the contexts in which reading takes place are conceived in similar ways (see Table 6.3 above) with a broadly comparable distribution of items by type of context.

6

RELATIONSHIP BETWEEN THE SURVEY OF ADULT SKILLS (PIAAC) AND THE OECD PROGRAMME FOR INTERNATIONAL STUDENT ASSESSMENT (PISA)

Response formats

The two assessments differ in terms of the format in which test-takers respond to test items. In the adult reading assessment, respondents provide answers by highlighting sections of text (selected response) in the computer-based version of the assessment, or by writing answers (constructed response) in the appropriate location in the paper-based version. The PISA reading assessment uses a wider variety of response formats, including standard multiple choice, complex multiple choice (where several selected response tasks have to be completed for a correct response), simple constructed response (where there is a single correct answer) and complex constructed response (where there are many possible ways to state the correct answer).

Numeracy

Table 6.4 provides a summary of the definition and the content, processes and context dimensions of the numeracy framework of the Survey of Adult Skills and the mathematical literacy framework for PISA. The similarities and differences are explored in more detail below.

Table 6.4 **Comparison of the Survey of Adult Skills (PIAAC) and PISA: Numeracy**

	Survey of Adult Skills (PIAAC)	**PISA**
Definition	The ability to access, use, interpret and communicate mathematical information and ideas, in order to engage in and manage the mathematical demands of a range of situations in adult life.	The capacity to identify and understand the role that mathematics plays in the world, to make well-founded judgements and to use and engage with mathematics in ways that meet the needs of that individual's life as a constructive, concerned and reflective citizen.
Content	Quantity and number Dimension and shape Pattern, relationships, change Data and chance	Quantity Space and shape Change and relationships
Cognitive processes	Identify, locate or access Act upon and use (order, count, estimate, compute, measure, model) Interpret, evaluate and analyse Communicate	Reproduction (simple mathematical operations) Connections (bringing together ideas to solve straightforward problems) Reflection (wider mathematical thinking)
Contexts	Everyday life Work-related Community and society Education and training	Personal Educational and occupational Public Scientific

Content

Both assessments cover closely related content areas in mathematical literacy/numeracy (e.g. "dimension and shape" in the Survey of Adult Skills and "space and shape" in PISA). The spread of items across the content areas is very similar in both assessments, although the Survey of Adult Skills puts a slightly greater emphasis on "quantity and number" than on "pattern, relationships and change". The content descriptions in the PISA frameworks include more knowledge of formal mathematical content than do those of the Survey of Adult Skills. Some items in PISA require formal, school-based mathematics (e.g. identify the gradient of a linear equation), while this type of knowledge is not required in the Survey of Adult Skills. PISA and the survey also differ slightly in the breadth of content they cover. As PISA measures the skills of 15-year-old students only, it focuses on secondary school-level mathematics. In contrast, the Survey of Adult Skills assesses skills across the entire adult population and, as a result, includes items that assume low levels of completed schooling (e.g. the early primary years). For example, some of the easiest items in PISA require comparing and interpreting data in complex tables of values, which include numbers into the tens and hundreds of thousands. In the Survey of Adult Skills, one of the easiest items requires recognising the smallest number in a one-column table of numbers less than one hundred.

6

RELATIONSHIP BETWEEN THE SURVEY OF ADULT SKILLS (PIAAC) AND THE OECD PROGRAMME FOR INTERNATIONAL STUDENT ASSESSMENT (PISA)

Cognitive processes

The cognitive processes respondents are expected to display are similar in the two assessments. However, unlike in content areas and contexts, the two sets of classifications do not match exactly. One difference is that the Survey of Adult Skills framework includes "communicate" as a category of cognitive process. However, due to the move to computer-based assessments, few items in the survey were classified as belonging to the category of "communicate" in the final assessment.

Contexts

A key feature of both assessments is that proficiency is assessed through problems set in context. Both assessments identify four contexts, with an approximately equal spread of items across each context. The four categories of context are similar in the respective frameworks (e.g. "everyday life" in the Survey of Adult Skills is very similar to "private" in PISA). The category of "education and training" in the survey does not exactly mirror the category of "scientific" contexts in PISA, but there is still a considerable overlap between them. The minor differences between the contexts used in the two frameworks reflect differences in the ages of the target groups for the assessments.

Representation and reading demands

PISA and the Survey of Adult Skills use a similar range of forms to convey mathematical information in real-life situations. These include, for example, objects to be counted (e.g. people, cars), symbolic notation (e.g. letters, operation signs), diagrams and tables. Texts may also play an important role, either by containing mathematical information in a textual form (e.g. "five" instead of "5", "crime rate increased by half") or by containing additional information that needs to be interpreted as part of the context. In both the survey and PISA 2012 there was an effort to reduce reading demands to distinguish performance in numeracy more clearly from the other measures of literacy. In both assessments this was achieved by minimising the amount of text and making it less complex, as well as by using supporting photos, images and illustrations. Most items are similar in reading demands, although PISA contains some items with more complex text (e.g. with formal mathematical terminology), while the Survey of Adult Skills includes items with very little text. This reflects the differences in the breadth of content assessed by the two surveys, as described above.

Item formats

There are some differences between PISA and the Survey of Adult Skills in the range of item types used; these are due to some operational constraints for the survey. Given its computer-based adaptive approach, the survey used short, separate tasks and selected-response (multiple choice) items. This still allowed respondents to answer in different modes (e.g. choosing from a pull-down menu, clicking on an area of the screen), but limited the capacity of the survey to assess communication-related skills (e.g. describing one's analysis of a situation). PISA used a wider range of formats, with both constructed-response and selected-response items. In addition, the optional computer-based component of PISA also used some interactive items (e.g. animation).

Complexity schemes

The frameworks for the Survey of Adult Skills and PISA contain a scheme describing the factors that affect item complexity. These schemes were used for different purposes, including designing items and describing performance levels. The survey scheme contains factors that consider the textual and mathematical aspects of complexity separately. Textual aspects include, for example, whether the problem is obvious or hidden. Mathematical aspects include, for example, the complexity of the data presented and how many operations respondents are expected to perform. The framework for PISA approaches complexity from a different angle. Its complexity scheme is based on a set of mathematical capabilities that underpin mathematical modelling (e.g. mathematising, reasoning and argument, using symbols, and devising strategies for solving problems).

Problem solving

Table 6.5 provides a summary of the definition and the content, processes and context dimensions of the problem solving framework in technology-rich environments of the Survey of Adult Skills and the problem-solving frameworks for PISA 2003 and 2012 (OECD, 2004, 2013).

Of the three domains discussed in this chapter, problem solving is the one where there is least relationship between the constructs assessed. In particular, the domain of problem solving in technology-rich environments and problem solving in PISA 2003 and 2012 conceive the 'content' dimension of their respective constructs in very different ways. The Survey of Adult Skills integrates a technology dimension not present in the PISA 2003 framework. Problem solving in PISA 2012 includes a technology dimension. However, this is conceived in different ways in the Survey of Adult Skills and PISA 2012. In particular, the technology dimension is instantiated in PISA 2012 in the form of simulated devices such as a MP3 player or air-conditioning system. In the Survey of Adult Skills, the technology dimension is present in the form of different

6

RELATIONSHIP BETWEEN THE SURVEY OF ADULT SKILLS (PIAAC) AND THE OECD PROGRAMME FOR INTERNATIONAL STUDENT ASSESSMENT (PISA)

applications (e.g. web browsers, webpages, email, spreadsheets) through which the information necessary to solve the problem situation is presented and which test-takers must use to solve the problem. In addition, the problem situation is conceived in different terms in the three studies – in relation to complexity and explicitness in the Survey of Adult Skills and by type of problem in PISA 2003 and in terms of interactive and static problems in PISA 2012.

Table 6.5 **Comparison of the Survey of Adult Skills (PIAAC) and PISA: Problem solving**

	Survey of Adult Skills (PIAAC)	PISA 2003	PISA 2012
Definition	The ability to use digital technology, communication tools and networks to acquire and evaluate information, communicate with others and perform practical tasks. The assessment focuses on the ability to solve problems for personal, work and civic purposes by setting up appropriate goals and plans, and accessing and making use of information through computers and computer networks.	An individual's capacity to use cognitive processes to confront and resolve real cross-disciplinary situations in which the solution path is not immediately obvious and where the literacy domains or curricular areas that might be applicable are within a single domain of science, mathematics or reading.	An individual's capacity to engage in cognitive processing to understand and resolve problem situations where a method of solution is not immediately obvious. It includes the willingness to engage with such situations in order to achieve one's potential as a constructive and reflective citizen.
Content	Technology: ▪ Hardware devices ▪ Software applications ▪ Commands and functions ▪ Representations (e.g. text, graphics, video) Nature of problems: ▪ *Intrinsic complexity*, which includes the number of steps required for solution, the number of alternatives, complexity of computation and/or transformation, number of constraints ▪ *Explicitness of the problem statement*, for example, largely unspecified or described in detail	Problem types: ▪ Decision making ▪ System analysis and design ▪ Trouble shooting	Problem solving situations: ▪ Static problem situations ▪ Interactive problem situations
Cognitive processes	Setting goals and monitoring progress Planning Acquiring and evaluating information Using information	Understanding Characterising Representing Reflecting Solving Communicating	Exploring and understanding Representing and formulating Planning and executing Monitoring and reflecting
Contexts	Personal Work and occupation Civic	Personal life Work and leisure Community and society	Setting: Technological or non-technological Focus: Personal or social

CONCLUSION

In sum, the Survey of Adult Skills and PISA share a similar broad approach to assessment and there is considerable commonality in the way in which the skills of literacy/reading literacy and numeracy/mathematical literacy are conceptualised and defined in the two studies. The overlap is greater in the case of literacy and reading literacy. The differences between the two studies in these domains relate, at least in part, to the different target populations: adults in the case of the Survey of Adult Skills, and 15-year-old students in the case of PISA. At least in the domains of literacy/reading and numeracy/mathematics, the Survey of Adult Skills and PISA can be regarded as measuring much the same skills in much the same way. At the same time, different measures are used in the two studies. The literacy and the numeracy scales used in the Survey of Adult Skills are not the same as their counterparts in PISA. While it would be expected that a high performer in reading literacy in PISA would be a relatively high performer in the Survey of Adult Skills, it is not possible to identify with any accuracy where a 15-year-old with a particular reading literacy or mathematics score in PISA would be located on the literacy or numeracy scales of the Survey of Adult Skills. In the absence of evidence from a study linking the two assessments, caution is advised in comparing the results of the two assessments.

6

RELATIONSHIP BETWEEN THE SURVEY OF ADULT SKILLS (PIAAC) AND THE OECD PROGRAMME FOR INTERNATIONAL STUDENT ASSESSMENT (PISA)

Notes

1. Fifteen-year-olds in home schooling may constitute an exception.

2. Some block-order effects (responses were affected by where the items were placed in the assessment) were found in respect of the IALS items in PISA that were not present in IALS.

3. This reflects the influence of the IALS frameworks on the development of both the PISA literacy framework (see OECD, 1999) and the literacy framework of the Survey of Adult Skills (PIAAC).

4. The discussion of the similarities and differences between the assessment frameworks underpinning the assessment of literacy/reading literacy and numeracy/mathematical literacy in the Survey of Adult Skills (PIAAC) draws on the work of Jones and Gabrielsen (forthcoming), and Gal and Tout (2014).

5. Multiple texts dominate in the electronic reading assessment of PISA.

References

Bushnik, T., L. Barr-Telford and P. Bussière (2003), *In and Out of High School: First Results from the Second Cycle of the Youth in Transition Survey, 2002*, Statistics Canada and Human Resources and Skills Development Canada, Ottawa.

Fullarton, S., M. Walker, J. Ainley and **K. Hillman** (2003) *Patterns of Participation in Year 12*, Longitudinal Surveys of Australian Youth Research Report 33, ACER, Camberwell, www.lsay.edu.au/publications/1857.html.

Gal, I. and **D. Tout** (2014), "Comparison of PIAAC and PISA Frameworks for Numeracy and Mathematical Literacy", *OECD Education Working Papers,* No. 102, OECD Publishing, Paris, http://dx.doi.org/10.1787/5jz3wl63cs6f-en.

Jones, S. and **E. Gabrielsen** (forthcoming), *Comparison of the Frameworks for Reading (PISA) and Literacy (PIAAC)*.

OECD (2013), *PISA 2012 Assessment and Analytical Framework: Mathematics, Reading, Science, Problem Solving and Financial Literacy*, OECD Publishing, Paris, http://dx.doi.org/10.1787/9789264190511-en.

OECD (2010a), *PISA 2009 Results: Learning Trends: Changes in Student Performance Since 2000 (Volume V)*, OECD Publishing, Paris, http://dx.doi.org/10.1787/9789264091580-en.

OECD (2010b), *PISA 2009 Assessment Framework: Key Competencies in Reading, Mathematics and Science*, OECD Publishing, Paris, http://dx.doi.org/10.1787/9789264062658-en.

OECD (2004), *The PISA 2003 Assessment Framework: Mathematics, Reading, Science and Problem Solving Knowledge and Skills*, OECD Publishing, Paris, http://dx.doi.org/10.1787/9789264101739-en.

OECD (2002), *Reading for Change: Performance and Engagement across Countries: Results from PISA 2000*, OECD Publishing, Paris, http://dx.doi.org/10.1787/9789264099289-en.

OECD (1999), *Measuring Student Knowledge and Skills: A New Framework for Assessment*, OECD Publishing, Paris, http://dx.doi.org/10.1787/9789264173125-en.

Yamamoto, K. (2002), *Estimating PISA Students on the IALS Prose Literacy Scale*, www.oecd.org/edu/preschoolandschool/programmeforinternationalstudentassessmentpisa/33680659.pdf.

7

The Survey
of Adult Skills (PIAAC)
and "key competencies"

This chapter discusses the evolution of the concept of "key competencies" and how the Survey of Adult Skills (PIAAC) defines the term.

Over the past 30 years, there have been many exercises, at both national and international levels, that have identified sets of competencies (or skills)[1] that are considered to be essential for successful participation in the labour market and/or should be developed by education and training systems to prepare individuals for working life and for participation in education and training and civic life.

At the international level, examples of key competency frameworks include those developed by the DeSeCo[2] project (Rychen and Salganik, 2003), the European Union (European Commission, 2007) and the ATC21S[3] group (Binkley et al., 2010). Among the many national frameworks that have been developed, there are those of the Secretary's Commission on Achieving Necessary Skills in the United States (SCANS, 1991), Conference Board of Canada (n.d.), the Mayer Commission (Mayer, 1992) and Employability Skills Framework in Australia (DEEWR, 2012), among others.

As discussed in Chapter 1, the competencies assessed in the Survey of Adult Skills (PIAAC) are conceived as "key information-processing competencies". Given this shared terminology, it is important to clarify the relationship of the Survey of Adult Skills to the work on defining and identifying key competencies. Two points are made in this respect:

- The Survey of Adult Skills shares a similar conceptualisation of competencies/skills with much of the work on key competencies.

- There is considerable overlap between the skills/competencies identified in key competency frameworks and those that are the focus of the Survey of Adult Skills.

THE DEFINITION OF KEY COMPETENCIES

What is competency?

Most of the work on key competencies (or skills) conceives competency in "functional" terms. Competency is the capacity to generate appropriate performance: to marshal the resources (tools, knowledge, techniques) in a social context (which involves interacting with others, understanding expectations) to realise a goal that is appropriate to the context. Commonly, competency is described in terms of the application and use of knowledge and skills in common life situations as opposed to the mastery of a body of knowledge or a repertoire of techniques. To this end, competencies are commonly conceived as encompassing three dimensions: knowledge, skills and attitudes (beliefs, dispositions, values).

At this point, a comment on terminology is appropriate. The use of the terms "competency" and "skill" as described in the previous paragraph is by no means universally shared. Many frameworks use "skill" in both a broad sense (the capacity to act appropriately in context) and in a more narrow sense (e.g. as a technical capacity). The ACT21S framework (Binkley et al., 2010), for example, identifies a number of 21st-century skills ("skills" in a broad sense) described in terms of "knowledge", "skills" (in the narrow sense) and "attitudes/values/ethics". Additionally, the concept of "competency" is used in different ways in different contexts, sometimes by the same author or organisation. An example is provided by the European Commission. In the European Key Competencies for Lifelong Learning framework (European Commission, 2007), "competency" is defined as encompassing or combining "knowledge" and "skill" – i.e. "skill" is a dimension or aspect of "competency". In the European Qualifications Framework (European Commission, 2008), "knowledge", "skills" and "competency" are treated as distinct categories of learning outcomes – i.e. "skill" is not conceived as a component of "competency". In this chapter and the one that follows, a pragmatic approach is adopted regarding the use of these two terms. "Competencies" and "skills" are used interchangeably except where the authors or frameworks referred to use them in a specific sense.

What is a key competency or skill?

There are four main features common to key competencies. Key competencies:

- constitute a prerequisite for achieving the desired outcome or outcomes, e.g. for a "successful life and a well-functioning society" (Rychen and Salganik, 2003), as preparation for the (emerging) labour market (Mayer, 1992), or for "personal fulfilment, active citizenship, social cohesion and employability in a knowledge society" (European Commission, 2007)

- are relevant to all individuals[4]

- can be learned

- are generic or highly transferable competencies that are relevant to multiple social fields and work situations, as opposed to competencies that are of relevance in specific occupations, industries or types of activity.

Key competencies are thus "general" competencies in the sense of being relevant to all members of the working population and across all fields of economic and social activity. While the economic and social importance of "specific" competencies (skills related to specific rather than general-use technologies, discipline-specific or occupation-specific skills) is not denied, they are intentionally defined to be outside the scope of key competency frameworks.

The main area in which frameworks differ concerns the treatment of personal qualities, attributes and attitudes. Some frameworks include individual dispositions and attitudes either as a dimension of competency or as a type of competency. For example, SCANS includes the personal qualities of individual responsibility, self-esteem, sociability, self-management, and integrity as part of its "foundation". The European Key Competencies for Lifelong Learning define appropriate attitudes in respect of each of its constituent domains of competency.[5] Other frameworks explicitly exclude personal qualities, values and attitudes. For example, the Australian Mayer Committee excluded personal qualities from the list of the key competencies it identified on the grounds that the key competencies had to be able to be developed through education and training, should not be based on innate predispositions or adherence to any particular set of values, and could be measured by credible assessment (Mayer, 1992). The DeSeCo framework excluded personal qualities and values on the basis that they are not competencies in themselves but rather conditions of the development of competency (Rychen and Salganik, 2003).

The classificatory schemas used to present key competencies also vary. Some frameworks establish hierarchies of competencies. For example, SCANS differentiates "competencies" from "foundations" in its framework of "workforce know-how". The foundations (basic skills, thinking skills and personal qualities) represent the pre-conditions for the acquisition of the competencies. The framework developed for the ALL study distinguishes between foundation skills and other skills built on this foundation by differentiating "fully portable" skills from "largely portable" skills (Murray et al., 2005, p. 67). Others, such as the European Key Competencies for Lifelong Learning (European Commission, 2007) do not establish a hierarchical relationship between groups of competencies. Frameworks also differ in whether or not they establish performance levels. The frameworks of SCANS and Mayer define performance levels, for example, whereas DeSeCo, EC and ATC21S do not.

Despite differences in terminology and classification, there is considerable convergence between frameworks. Four broad groups of competencies are identified by most frameworks: cognitive competencies, interpersonal skills, intrapersonal competencies, and technological skills (usually related to the use of ICTs as a general use technology).[6] Within these broad groupings, subgroups are often identified. Table 7.1 provides an overview of the broad groupings of competencies and their constituent subcategories, and illustrates the subcategories with specific examples drawn from existing frameworks.

Table 7.1 Competency groups and examples of specific competencies in competency frameworks

Competency groups	Examples of specific competencies cited in frameworks
Cognitive competencies	
Communication	Reading, writing, oral communication, proficiency in foreign languages.
Information processing	Thinking skills, managing information.
Problem solving	Recognising problems and devising and implementing a plan of action, discovering a rule or principle underlying the relationship between two or more objects and applying it when solving a problem.
Learning	Learning to learn, reflexivity, effective management of one's own learning.
Mathematics	Using numbers, reasoning mathematically, communicating in mathematical language.
Interpersonal competencies	
Interpersonal	Team work, cultural sensitivity, working with others, relating to customers, negotiating, participate in projects and tasks.
Intrapersonal competencies	
Self-regulation	Self-awareness, reflexivity, meta-cognition, adaptability, coping with stress.
Management	Planning (self and others), organisation, responsibility.
Creativity/entrepreneurship	Initiative, creativity, ability to assess and take risks.
Technological competencies	
ICT	Work with a variety of technologies, use IT to organise data.

THE SURVEY OF ADULT SKILLS (PIAAC) AND KEY COMPETENCIES

How do the skills about which information is collected in the Survey of Adult Skills relate to the competencies commonly identified as "key competencies"?

First, the Survey of Adult Skills and most key competency frameworks share a functional conception. The focus of both is on generating performance that is appropriate to context.

Second, the skills directly assessed in the Survey of Adult Skills comprise core components in classifications of key competencies. Reading, numeracy and problem solving as well as the use of ICTs are explicitly identified as key skills (or competencies) in all competency frameworks. Table 7.2 provides a summary of the coverage of the broad domains of competency identified in Table 7.1 above, by both the direct measures and the questions relating to the use of skills in work and everyday life in the Survey of Adult Skills.

Table 7.2 **Key competencies and skills covered in the Survey of Adult Skills (PIAAC)**

Key competencies	Measured directly in the Survey of Adult Skills (PIAAC)	Measured indirectly (through self-reports) in the Survey of Adult Skills (PIAAC)
Cognitive competencies		
Communication	Literacy (reading)	Reading and writing (work and personal life)
Information processing		
Problem solving	Problem solving in technology-rich environments	Problem solving (work)
Learning		Learning activities (work) Deep learning
Mathematics	Numeracy	Numeracy activities (work and personal life)
Intra and interpersonal competencies		
Interpersonal		Collaboration, influencing (work) Trust in others
Self-regulation		Learning style
Management		Organisation/planning (work)
Creativity/entrepreneurship		
Technological competencies		
ICT	Literacy (digital reading), problem solving in technology-rich environments, ICT core test	ICT use (work, everyday life)

While the skills assessed in the Survey of Adult Skills feature in most key competency frameworks, they nevertheless represent a subset – albeit an important one – of the skills and competencies identified in competency frameworks. For example, the communication skills identified in competency frameworks go well beyond reading to encompass oral communication, written communication, and sometimes communication in a second language. The intra- and interpersonal competencies included in competency frameworks go well beyond the relatively narrow set of skills about which the Survey of Adult Skills collects information.

The Survey of Adult Skills was not designed to operationalise elements of any particular competency framework. The selection of the skills that are assessed in the survey, the definition of constructs, and the selection of skills about which information on use is collected are not based on the use or acceptance of any single framework.[7] In fact, the relationship between the reflection on key competencies and 21st-century skills that has been ongoing since the late 1980s, and the development of large-scale assessments of adults that has culminated in the Survey of Adult Skills, is a complex one. On the one hand, both the interest in measuring cognitive skills and the interest in identifying key competencies can be seen as having a common origin in the reflection on the direction and speed of technological change and economic restructuring and the growing importance of cross-cutting cognitive and non-cognitive skills in a high-skilled, service-based economy. On the other hand, work on key competencies and the development of skills assessments have not proceeded in isolation from each other; in fact, there has been considerable mutual influence.

 THE SURVEY OF ADULT SKILLS: READER'S COMPANION, SECOND EDITION

For example, the experience of large-scale international assessments of adults (in particular that of the International Adult Literacy Survey) and school students (PISA) and the approach to the definition of literacy competency in these studies provided an influential backdrop to the development of the DeSeCo framework. The DeSeCo framework was, in turn, influential in developing the Adult Literacy and Life Skills Survey, particularly in terms of exploring the possibility of extending the assessment beyond the domains of literacy and numeracy (OECD/Statistics Canada, 2005, p. 26). More recently, both PISA and the Survey of Adult Skills have provided points of reference for the work of the ATC21S group, particularly given the emphasis ATC21S places on IT skills and on assessment as an essential component of a framework defining 21st-century skills and describing 21st-century learning outcomes in a form that can facilitate measurement.

Notes

1. The nomenclature varies – "key competencies", "core skills", "essential skills", "21st-century skills" and "employability skills", for example, have all been used in different exercises. Despite attempts to distinguish "competencies" from "skills", the terms are used more or less interchangeably in practice.

2. Definition and Selection of Competencies.

3. Assessment and Teaching of 21st-Century Skills.

4. The Mayer Committee, for example, took the view that the key competencies that it identified were competencies that were so important that they "should be acquired by all young people in their preparation for work" (Mayer, 1992, p. ix).

5. As an example, "an entrepreneurial attitude is characterised by initiative, pro-activity, independence and innovation in personal and social life, as much as at work. It also includes motivation and determination to meet objectives, whether personal goals, or aims held in common with others, including at work" (European Commission, 2007).

6. This draws on meta-classifications of the skills identified by key competency frameworks in Curtis and McKenzie (2001), Murray et al. (2005, pp. 54-57), and Pellegrino and Hilton (2012, pp. 2-12–2-14).

7. Nor, might it be added, only in work relating to key competencies.

References

Binkley, M., O. Erstad, J. Herman, S. Raizen and M. Ripley (2010), *Defining 21st Century Skills*, ATC21S, http://cms.education.gov.il/NR/rdonlyres/19B97225-84B1-4259-B423-4698E1E8171A/115804/defining21stcenturyskills.pdf.

Conference Board of Canada (n.d.), *Employability Skills 2000+*, www.conferenceboard.ca/Libraries/EDUC_PUBLIC/esp2000.sflb.

Curtis, D. and P. McKenzie (2001), *Employability Skills for Australian Industry: Literature Review and Framework Development*, Australian Council for Educational Research, Melbourne.

DEEWR (Department of Education, Employment and Workplace Relations) (2012), *Employability Skills Framework Stage 1: Final Report*, Department of Education, Employment and Workplace Relations, Canberra, www.voced.edu.au/content/ngv%3A52686.

European Commission (2008), *The European Qualifications Framework for Lifelong Learning (EQF)*, Office for Official Publications of the European Communities, Luxembourg.

European Commission (2007), *Key Competencies for Lifelong Learning: European Reference Framework*, Office for Official Publications of the European Communities, Luxembourg.

Mayer, E. (Chairman) (1992), *Key Competencies: Report of the Committee to Advise the Australian Education Council and Ministers of Vocational Education, Employment and Training on Employment-related Key Competencies for Post-compulsory Education and Training*, Australian Education Council and Ministers of Vocational Education, Employment and Training, Canberra.

Murray, S., Y. Clermont and M. Binkley (eds.) (2005), *Measuring Adult Literacy and Life Skills: New Frameworks for Assessment*, Statistics Canada, Ottawa, Catalogue No. 89-552-MIE, No. 13.

OECD/Statistics Canada (2005), *Learning a Living: First Results of the Adult Literacy and Life Skills Survey*, OECD Publishing, Paris, http://dx.doi.org/10.1787/9789264010390-en.

Pellegrino, J. W. and M. L. Hilton (eds.) (2012), *Education for Life and Work: Developing Transferable Knowledge and Skills in the 21st Century*, National Academies Press, Washington, DC.

Rychen, D. and L. Salganik (eds.) (2003), *Key Competencies for a Successful Life and a Well-Functioning Society*, Hogrefe and Huber Publishers, Göttingen.

SCANS (The Secretary's Commission on Achieving Necessary Skills) (1991), *What Work Requires of Schools: A SCAN's Report for America*, US Department of Labor, Washington, DC.

8

The Survey of Adult Skills (PIAAC) and the measurement of human capital

This chapter briefly discusses the concept of "human capital" and examines the extent to which the Survey of Adult Skills (PIAAC) assesses some of its components. It also compares the strengths and weaknesses of using direct measures of skills, such as those afforded by the Survey of Adult Skills, with those of using educational attainment to assess human capital.

Robust, internationally comparable measures of the proficiency of adults in cognitive skills such as literacy, numeracy and problem solving arguably have the potential to provide better proxy measures of human capital than commonly used measures, such as educational attainment or years of schooling, as well as providing important information in themselves. In 1998, a report on the measurement of human capital, *Human Capital Investment*, prepared by the OECD Centre for Educational Research and Innovation (CERI) concluded that: "To achieve a better understanding and measurement of human capital, it is necessary to develop direct measures of skill, competency and aptitudes, as well as the broad social and economic impact of human capital" (OECD, 1998, p. 81). In line with this conclusion, Hanushek and Woessman, in particular (see, for example, Woessman, 2003; Hanushek and Woessmann, 2009; and Hanushek, and Woessman, 2011), have argued that the results from international assessments of school students, such as PISA and Trends in International Mathematics and Science Study (TIMSS) (and results of adult surveys where they exist), constitute good measures of human capital and have considerable advantages over quantity-based measures, particularly completed years of schooling, at least in growth-accounting studies.

This chapter explores the extent to which it is legitimate to interpret the skills assessed in the Survey of Adult Skills (PIAAC) as (proxy) measures of human capital, the advantages and disadvantages of direct measures of key information-processing skills and measures based on educational qualifications as measures of human capital and, the ways in which these direct measures complement traditional measures to enhance the quality of indicators of human capital.

DEFINING "HUMAN CAPITAL"

In considering the value of direct measures of cognitive skills as a measure of human capital, it is important first to define "human capital". A useful definition is provided by OECD (1998), which defines human capital as "the knowledge, skills, competencies and other attributes embodied in individuals that are relevant to economic activity" (OECD, 1998, p. 9). The dimensions of human capital identified in the OECD definition are described in more detail in Table 8.1, drawing on the descriptions of similar concepts found in the competency literature.[1]

Table 8.1 **Components of human capital**

Component	Description
Knowledge	The body of facts, principles, theories and practices relevant to a field of work or study.
Skills	The ability to apply knowledge and use know-how to complete tasks and solve problems. Skills are commonly further classified into: • cognitive skills • technical skills • interpersonal and intrapersonal skills • communication skills.
Competency/Application	The ability to use knowledge and skills appropriately in real-life contexts and situations. Competency is often conceived in terms of capacity to exercise responsibility and act autonomously.
Personal attributes	The personality traits, behavioural dispositions and physical characteristics, such as strength, manual dexterity, height or even personal appearance, which may have a value on the labour market.

The components of human capital may be further specified in that knowledge, skills, competencies and attributes may be broadly transferable (or generic) in that they are relevant in a wide variety of situations (e.g. in different occupations and in different firms). Alternatively, they may be transferable to a limited extent or relevant in a limited set of situations (e.g. specific to an occupation or a particular enterprise) or related to a particular domain of knowledge or activity.

COVERAGE OF THE DIMENSIONS OF HUMAN CAPITAL IN THE SURVEY OF ADULT SKILLS (PIAAC)

To what extent do educational qualifications and the measures provided by the Survey of Adult Skills cover the various dimensions of human capital as outlined in above?

Table 8.2 locates the skills assessed directly by the Survey of Adult Skills in a matrix defined in one dimension by the components of human capital and in the other by the degree of their transferability.

Table 8.2 **Coverage of the dimensions of human capital directly assessed in the Survey of Adult Skills (PIAAC)**

	Broadly transferable	Less transferable
Knowledge	Assessed to a limited extent (literacy and numeracy)	Not assessed
Skills (cognitive)	Assessed (literacy, numeracy and problem solving)	Not assessed
Skills (technical)	Assessed to a limited extent (computer use)	Not assessed
Skills (inter and intra-personal)	Not assessed	Not assessed
Competency/Application	Not assessed	Not assessed
Personal attributes	Not assessed	Not assessed

The direct-assessment component of the Survey of Adult Skills focuses on measuring three cognitive skills (literacy, numeracy and problem solving in technology-rich environments) that are broadly transferable (generic) in nature. As is clear from the way these skills are defined in their frameworks (see Chapter 1), the assessment's interest in these skills is centred on the *application* of knowledge and know-how in contexts that are relevant to adults generally. Content knowledge and technical skills represent a secondary focus of the assessment. A relatively limited amount of information is provided concerning respondents' content *knowledge* (e.g. knowledge of basic mathematical concepts and operations in the case of numeracy). Some information is also provided regarding the mastery of certain *technical skills* (e.g. the capacity to use basic computer devices, commands, functions and applications) by the ICT core test and the problem-solving assessment, which assumes a basic level of skills in the use of applications and functionalities, such as e-mail, word processing, and spreadsheets.

Neither inter- and intra-personal skills nor personal attitudes are the object of direct assessment in the Survey of Adult Skills, even if questions are asked about the use of some inter- and intra-personal skills at work. Domain-specific skills (e.g. specific vocational or professional skills, firm-specific skills and knowledge related to particular fields of study) are also outside the scope of the survey, as is the extent to which individuals can act autonomously (competency).

The Survey of Adult Skills' focus on assessing a small number of broadly transferable cognitive skills reflects both the importance attributed to measuring literacy, numeracy and problem solving in technology-rich environments as key information-processing skills, and the limits on what can be measured in a large-scale, international adult assessment given the current state of measurement science, the need to minimise the burden on respondents, and the amount of resources that can be reasonably be expected to be devoted to this type of exercise.

Direct measurement of inter- and intra-personal skills poses considerable methodological challenges in large-scale, cross-country surveys. These relate to both the definition of constructs and the methods of measurement. For example, what is considered to be the appropriate form of interaction between colleagues and superiors and, therefore, what behaviours define a concept such as "teamwork" are likely to vary between countries, given different cultural expectations and norms. Moreover, it is not obvious that individual survey-based approaches are effective for measuring inter- and intra-personal skills. These may be better assessed through observation or by using the judgements of the subject's behaviour and interpersonal interactions by colleagues and/or supervisors. In the Adult Literacy and Life Skills Survey (ALL), for example, a framework for measuring teamwork was developed but not implemented as it was judged to be not sufficiently robust for a large-scale, cross-country assessment (see Murray et al., 2005, pp. 229-270). For the moment at least, information on inter- and intra-personal skills must be collected through indirect methods of the type used in the Survey of Adult Skills, whatever their limitations.[2]

Scales such as the "big Five", "locus of control" and "grit" exist for measuring personality traits and behavioural dispositions. The "big Five" consists of an inventory of questions relating to five traits considered to represent personality at the broadest level of abstraction (see John and Srivastava, 2001): extraversion, agreeableness, conscientiousness, neuroticism, and openness to experience. "Locus of control" relates to beliefs about the extent to which life's outcomes are under the subject's own control as opposed to being determined by factors beyond his/her control. Individuals with an internal locus of control generally believe that life's outcomes are due to their own efforts, while those with an external locus of control believe that outcomes are mainly due to external factors (Gatz and Karel, 1993). "Grit" relates to "perseverance and passion for long-term goals", in other words, attributes related to "working strenuously toward challenges, maintaining effort and interest over years despite failure, adversity, and plateaus in progress" (Duckworth et al., 2007).

The "big Five" and "locus of control" inventories have been used to measure non-cognitive and personality traits in large-scale surveys such as the Household, Income and Labour Dynamics in Australia (HILDA) Survey (see HILDA, n.d.) and the German Panel survey (Headey and Holst, 2008). As noted in Chapter 5, both the "big Five" and "grit" scales are being administered as part of the World Bank's STEP measurement study. Items relating to "locus of control" and "grit" were included in the field-test version of the Survey of Adult Skills background questionnaire. They were, however, dropped for the main study due to evidence of lack of comparability between countries.

There has also been work on assessing vocational, domain-specific skills and knowledge using large-scale survey techniques in an international context (see Baethge and Arends, 2009). The OECD completed a feasibility study on the Assessment of Higher Education Learning Outcomes (AHELO) in 2013, which investigated the feasibility of conducting an international assessment of university students that focuses on discipline-specific skills in economics and engineering as well as a set of generic skills (critical thinking, analytical reasoning, problem solving and written communication). The main issue regarding the measurement of domain-specific skills is less whether they can be validly and reliably measured in a cross-country context – which the AHELO feasibility study demonstrated to be possible – than the practicality and costs of measurement using household-survey methods, given their number and variety.

EDUCATIONAL ATTAINMENT AS A MEASURE OF HUMAN CAPITAL

Educational attainment (or its variants, such as years of schooling) represents the most commonly used summary measure of human capital. This is due to its ready availability (information on educational qualifications is collected in most social surveys), the importance of qualifications as a signal of skills in the labour market, and the fact that educational qualifications provide a considerable amount of information regarding the breadth and depth of the knowledge, skills and competency of the individuals to which they have been awarded.[3] The role and importance of formal education and training in the development of individuals' store of knowledge and skills can hardly be disputed.

A good overview, albeit at a reasonably high level of generality, of the information summarised by the award of different educational qualifications can be gained by examining the descriptors of qualifications offered by national (and cross-national) qualifications frameworks. First, qualifications certify a broad range of learning outcomes. A common "horizontal" classification of the types of learning outcomes that education programmes are expected to impart and that graduates of these programmes are expected to display used in qualifications frameworks is that of "knowledge", "skills" and "competency" (European Commission, 2008) or some variation of this.[4] Second, qualifications offer information on the depth of knowledge and skills that graduates are expected to have acquired. Typically, qualifications frameworks group qualifications in terms of "levels"[5] that represent stages in an ordered progression of the complexity and depth of knowledge and skills different educational programmes are intended to impart and that their "graduates" are, therefore, expected to display.

Taking the descriptors used in national and cross-national frameworks (e.g. the European Qualifications Framework) as a guide, educational qualifications can be regarded as offering relatively comprehensive measures of human capital in that they provide information about individuals' stocks of both broadly transferable and less transferable knowledge, skills and competency (Table 8.3). They also provide information on the complexity and depth of these skills. The extent to which they cover any of the particular cells in the table will depend on the nature of the qualification. For example, vocationally oriented qualifications will certify the existence of skills with limited transferability to a far greater extent than will a general qualification, such as a certificate of senior secondary education.

Table 8.3 **Coverage of the dimensions of human capital by educational qualifications**

	Broadly transferable	**Transferable to a limited extent**
Knowledge	low-high	low-high
Skills (cognitive)	low-high	low-high
Skills (technical)	low-high	low-high
Skills (inter and intra-personal)	low-high	low-high
Competency	low-high	low-high
Personal attributes	not covered	not covered

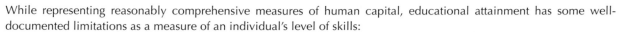

While representing reasonably comprehensive measures of human capital, educational attainment has some well-documented limitations as a measure of an individual's level of skills:

- Educational qualifications certify only the knowledge and skills developed through a course of study.[5] They, thus, provide information about a subset of the skills of an individual. However, as noted above, this is by no means a negligible component of an individual's skills, particularly in the case of young adults.

- An educational qualification certifies the achievement of certain learning outcomes at a particular point in time. The currency of the measure will depend on the period of time that has elapsed since the qualification was awarded, and the experience (professional and otherwise) of individuals during this period. Skills can be lost as well as maintained and enhanced over time.

- The quality of education and training offered at different levels of the education and training system can vary considerably between countries and, within countries, over time. Thus, the level of knowledge and skills certified by a qualification of ostensibly the same type and level may vary widely.

COMPARING MEASURES OF HUMAN CAPITAL

As can be seen from the above, direct measures of literacy, numeracy and problem solving in technology-rich environments and educational qualifications have different strengths and weaknesses as proxies of human capital or "global skills". A comparison of four criteria is presented in Table 8.4 below:

- Coverage – the extent to which the measure covers the different dimensions of human capital.

- Context dependence – the extent to which the measure covers skills learned in a particular context, such as an educational institution.

- Currency – the extent to which the measure is "up-to-date" as a measure of skills at the date information is collected.

- Comparability – the extent to which the measure is comparable across countries and across time within countries.

Table 8.4 **Comparison of direct measures from the Survey of Adult Skills (PIAAC) and qualifications on four criteria**

	Direct assessment (Survey of Adult Skills)	Qualifications
Coverage (content)	Limited (only 3 cognitive skills tested)	Broad
Context dependence	Low	High
Currency	High	Variable (depends on the time elapsed since the respondent's highest qualification was completed)
Comparability	High	Variable both between and within countries

The Survey of Adult Skills' direct measures provide detailed information about a narrow range of the skills that is highly current, not related to any particular context of acquisition, and is highly comparable within and between countries/economies. Qualifications provide information about most of the dimensions of human capital, but cover only those skills developed through formal education and training, are of varying currency (most current for the young and least current for the old), and are of sometimes dubious comparability.

EMPIRICAL EVIDENCE

Analysis of data from the Survey of Adult Skills, International Adult Literacy Survey (IALS) and ALL provides some empirical evidence relevant to the question of the value of direct measures of proficiency in information processing skills and educational attainment as indicators of human capital. First, direct measures and educational qualifications do not appear to measure the same underlying traits. While educational attainment and literacy proficiency, for example, are closely correlated, there is considerable variation evident in literacy proficiency among individuals with similar levels of attainment (see Chapter 5 of *OECD Skills Outlook* [OECD, 2013] and OECD/Statistics Canada, 2000 and 2011). Second, educational attainment and literacy proficiency each have an independent and positive impact on earnings (see Chapter 6 of *OECD Skills Outlook* [OECD, 2013], OECD/Statistics Canada, 2000, pp. 76-79; OECD/Statistics Canada, 2011).

ENHANCING THE MEASUREMENT OF HUMAN CAPITAL

In sum, direct measures of skills are best seen as offering an important complement to the indirect measures of human capital provided by educational attainment rather than as a substitute for them. By providing information both on educational attainment and proficiency in literacy, numeracy and problem solving in technology-rich environments, the Survey of Adult Skills offers greater insight into the human capital endowments of individuals and nations than would otherwise be available. Linked to the fact that it covers more countries/economies than previous adult skills surveys, measures new domains of skills and, in some countries/economies, provides for comparisons with previous surveys, the Survey of Adult Skills should offer a more accurate picture of skills relevant to the labour market and could help to explain differences in earnings and economic growth.

Notes

1. See the previous chapter for a discussion of the uses of the terms "skill" and "competency".

2. These are well known. First, while it can be inferred from the fact that a person undertakes certain tasks at work that he/she possesses the skills necessary to undertake these tasks to a greater or lesser extent, the level of his/her proficiency in these skills cannot be accurately inferred. Second, the degree of overlap between what people are required to do at work and what they can do is not necessarily particularly high. It is likely that many, if not most, adults possess the skills to effectively perform many tasks that they are not required to undertake at work.

3. Barro and Lee (2010) argue that at the macro-level, accurate time series of years of schooling (based on attainment measures) can be developed for most countries and that these provide a reasonable proxy for the stock of human capital in a broad range of countries.

4. The Australian Qualifications Framework Council (2013) defines three dimensions of learning outcomes: knowledge, skills and application. The Scottish Credit and Qualifications Framework (SCQF, n.d) defines five classes of learning outcomes: knowledge and understanding (mainly subject-based); practice (applied knowledge and understanding); generic cognitive skills (e.g. evaluation, critical analysis); communication, numeracy and IT skills; and autonomy, accountability and working with others.

5. See, for example, the explanation of "levels" in the International Standard Classification of Education (ISCED): "The notion of "levels" of education is represented by an ordered set of categories, intended to group educational programmes in relation to gradations of learning experiences and the knowledge, skills and competencies which each programme is designed to impart" (UNESCO, 2011, p. 10).

6. With the exception of awarding qualifications based on the recognition of prior learning (RPL). Qualifications awarded on the basis of RPL represent a minute proportion of the qualifications held by the adult population.

References

Australian Qualifications Framework Council (2013), *Australian Qualifications Framework Second Edition January 2013*, www.aqf.edu.au/wp-content/uploads/2013/05/AQF-2nd-Edition-January-2013.pdf.

Baethge, M. and **L. Arends** (2009), *Feasibility Study VET-LSA: A Comparative Analysis of Occupational Profiles and VET Programmes in 8 European Countries: International Report*, Federal Ministry of Education and Research, Bonn.

Barro, R.J. and **J.-W. Lee** (2010), "A New Data Set of Educational Attainment in the World, 1950-2010", *NBER Working Paper* No. 1590, www.nber.org/papers/w15902.pdf?new_window=1.

Duckworth, A.L., C. Peterson, M.D. Matthews and **D.R. Kelly** (2007), "Grit: Perseverance and Passion for Long-Term Goals", *Journal of Personality and Social Psychology*, Vol. 92, No. 6, pp. 1087-1101.

European Commission (EC) (2008), *The European Qualifications Framework for Lifelong Learning (EQF)*, Office for Official Publications of the European Communities, Luxembourg.

Gatz, M. and **J. Karel** (1993), "Individual Change in Perceived Control over 20 Years", *International Journal of Behavioral Development*, No. 16, pp. 305-322.

Hanushek, E.A. and **L. Woessmann** (2011), "The Economics of International Differences in Educational Achievement", in E.A. Hanushek, S. Machin and L. Woessmann (eds), *Handbooks in Economics*, Vol. 3, The Netherlands, pp. 89-200.

Hanushek, E.A. and **L. Woessmann** (2009), "Do Better Schools Lead to More Growth? Cognitive Skills, Economic Outcomes, and Causation", *NBER Working Paper*, No. 14633, www.nber.org/papers/w14633.pdf?new_window=1.

Headey, B. and **E. Holst (eds.)** (2008), *A Quarter Century of Change: Results from the German Socio-Economic Panel (SOEP)*, DIW, Berlin.

Household of Income and Labour Dynamics Australia Survey (HILDA) (n.d.), HILDA Website: www.melbourneinstitute.com/hilda/.

John, O. and **S. Srivastava** (2001), "The Big-Five Trait Taxonomy: History, Measurement, and Theoretical Perspectives", in L. Pervin, O. John (Eds.), *Handbook of Personality: Theory and Research*, Chap. 4, Guilford Press, New York, 2nd ed., pp. 102-138.

Murray, S., Y. Clermont and **M. Binkley (eds.)** (2005), *Measuring Adult Literacy and Life Skills: New Frameworks for Assessment*, Statistics Canada, Ottawa, Catalogue No. 89-552-MIE, No. 13.

OECD (2013), *OECD Skills Outlook 2013: First Results from the Survey of Adult Skills*, OECD Publishing, Paris, http://dx.doi.org/10.1787/9789264204256-en.

OECD (1998), *Human Capital Investment: An international Comparison*, OECD Publishing, Paris, http://dx.doi.org/10.1787/9789264162891-en.

OECD/Statistics Canada (2011), *Literacy for Life: Further Results from the Adult Literacy and Life Skills Survey*, OECD Publishing, Paris, http://dx.doi.org/10.1787/9789264091269-en.

OECD/Statistics Canada (2000), *Literacy in the Information Age: Final Report of the International Adult Literacy Survey*, OECD Publishing, Paris, http://dx.doi.org/10.1787/9789264181762-en.

Scottish Credit and Qualifications Framework (SCQF) (n.d.), Scottish Credit and Qualifications Framework Website: www.scqf.org.uk/The%20Framework/Level%20Descriptors.

UNESCO (2011), *Revision of the International Standard Classification of Education (ISCED)*, Paper 36 C/19, 34th Session of the General Conference, 2011, UNESCO, www.uis.unesco.org/Education/Documents/UNESCO_GC_36C-19_ISCED_EN.pdf.

Woessmann, L. (2003), "Specifying Human Capital", *Journal of Economic Surveys*, Vol. 17, No. 3, pp. 239-270.

Annex A

**Relationship between the level of descriptors
used in the Survey of Adult Skills (PIAAC)
and other skills surveys**

In presenting the results of the Survey of Adult Skills (PIAAC), the descriptors used to describe the characteristics of the tasks at each proficiency level in literacy and numeracy differ from those used when presenting the results of the International Adult Literacy Survey (IALS) and the Adult Literacy and Life Skills Survey (ALL). This is the result of:

- The introduction of the domain of *literacy*, which replaces the previously separate domains of prose and document literacy used in IALS and ALL.

- A change in the way in which the "proficiency" of individuals and the "difficulty" of items are defined in the Survey of Adult Skills compared to the IALS and ALL.

A single literacy scale

The construct of "literacy" measured in the Survey of Adult Skills encompasses prose and document literacy, which were reported on separate scales in previous international adult literacy surveys, and also incorporates the reading of digital texts. Irrespective of any change to the definition of proficiency levels, the development of a new, single literacy scale necessitated a review of the descriptors of the proficiency levels used for reporting results.

The definition of proficiency levels

The Survey of Adult Skills locates items and individuals on the three proficiency scales using a response probability (RP) value of 0.67. In other words, individuals are located on the scale at the point at which he or she has a 67% probability of successfully completing a random set of items representing the construct measured. Items are located on the scale at the point at which they have a 67% probability of being successfully completed by a random sample of the adult population. This differs from the approach used in IALS and ALL in which a response probability of 0.80 was used. This change was made so that the approach used to define what it means for a person to be at a certain proficiency level was similar to that used in PISA (see OECD, 2010, p. 48).

The change in response probability has no consequences for either the estimation of the proficiency or the precision of the scales. The estimation of proficiency is independent of the selection of an RP value, as it is a function of the level of correct response to the test items. The precision of the scale is a function of the number of items in the scale, which is again independent of the choice of RP value. What the change in RP value does affect is the way proficiency is defined and described. In effect, "proficiency" is defined in terms of a different probability of successfully completing tasks. In the case of the shift from an RP value of 0.80 to one of 0.67, the result is that proficiency is described in terms of more **difficult** items that are completed with a **lower probability** of success.

This can be seen in the Table A.1 below, which presents item maps for literacy and numeracy when response probabilities of 0.67 and 0.80 are used. For example, the literacy item "Summer Streets" is located at 350 on the scale when a response probability of 0.67 is used as opposed to 369 when 0.80 is used. Similarly, the numeracy item "TV" moves from 279 to 260 when the response probability changes from 0.67 to 0.80.

[Part 1/2]

Table A.1 **Location of items on the literacy scale using RP67 and RP80**

Score	RP67	RP80
400		Baltic Stock Market C308A116
398		Library Search C323P005
397		CANCO 306B111
389		Work-related Stress C329P003
386		Apples *P317P001*
376	Library Search C323P005	Work-related Stress C329P002
374	Work-related Stress C329P003	
372	CANCO C306B111	
371	Baltic Stock Market C308A116	
369		Summer Streets C327P004
368		Milk Label *P324P002*
364		Library Search C323P002
359	Apples *P317P001*	
358		Baltic Stock Market C308A118
357		Generic Medicines C309A322
350	Summer Streets C327P004	
349	Work-related Stress C329P002	
348	Library Search C323P002	
347	Milk Label *P324P002*	
346		Distances-Mexican Cities C315B512
343		Library Search C323P004
342		Summer Streets C327P003
341		International Calls C313A410
337	Baltic Stock Market C308A118	
336		Milk Label *P324P003*
333		Civil Engineering C318P003
331		Contact Employer C304B711
330		Summer Streets C327P002
329	Generic Medicines C309A322 Library Search C323P004	International Calls C313A411 Memory Training C310A407 TMN Anti-theft C305A218

...

[Part 2/2]

Table A.1 **Location of items on the literacy scale using RP67 and RP80**

Score	RP67	RP80
324	International Calls C313A410	
321		
320	Summer Streets C327P003	Summer Streets C327P001
318	Distances-Mexican Cities C315B512	Civil Engineering C318P001
316	Civil Engineering C318P003	
315	International Calls C313A411	
314		Baltic Stock Market C308A119 Lakeside Fun Run C322P003
312	Memory Training C310A407	
312	Milk Label *P324P003*	
309	TMN Anti-theft C305A218	
308		Lakeside Fun Run C322P004 MEDCO Aspirin C307B402
306	Summer Streets C327P002	Lakeside Fun Run C322P001
305		Library Search C323P003 International Calls C313A413
304	Contact Employer C304B711	
303	Civil Engineering C318P001	
301		Discussion forum C320P003 Discussion forum C320P004
298	Summer Streets C327P001	Contact Employer C304B710
297	Baltic Stock Market C308A119	
295		Baltic Stock Market C308A121
294	Lakeside Fun Run C322P003	
293	Lakeside Fun Run C322P004	Discussion forum C320P001
292		International Calls C313A414
291		Generic Medicines C309A319
289	Library Search C323P003	
288	MEDCO Aspirin C307B402	
287		Apples *P317P003*
286	Discussion forum C320P003 International Calls C313A413 Contact Employer C304B710	Memory Training C310A406
285	Discussion forum C320P004	
283	Lakeside Fun Run C322P001	Apples *P317P002*
281	Discussion forum C320P001	
280		International Calls C313A412
280		Internet Poll C321P002
279	Baltic Stock Market C308A121	TMN Anti-theft C305A215
272	Memory Training C310A406 Generic Medicines C309A319 International Calls C313A414	Internet Poll C321P001
271		Baltic Stock Market C308A120
265	Apples *P317P003*	Lakeside Fun Run C322P002
264		Lakeside Fun Run C322P005
262	Apples *P317P002*	
261		CANCO C306B110
260	TMN Anti-theft C305A215	
259		Baltic Stock Market C308A117
258		Generic Medicines C309A320
257	International Calls C313A412	
254	Baltic Stock Market C308A120	
251	Internet Poll C321P001	
244	CANCO C306B110 Lakeside Fun Run C322P005	
240	Lakeside Fun Run C322P002	Generic Medicines C309A321
239	Baltic Stock Market C308A117	
239	Generic Medicines C309A320	
238	Internet Poll C321P002	
234		Guadeloupe *P330P001*
231		Dutch Women *C311B701*
219	Generic Medicines C309A321	
207	Guadeloupe *P330P001*	
203		Election Results *C302BC02*
201	Dutch Women *C311B701*	
190		MEDCO Aspirin *C30B7401*
169	MEDCO Aspirin *C30B7401*	
163		Employment Ad *C300AC02*
162	Election Results *C302BC02*	
136	Employment Ad *C300AC02*	
117		SGIH *C301AC05*
75	SGIH *C301AC05*	

[Part 1/2]

Table A.2 Location of items on the numeracy scale using RP67 and RP80

Score	RP67		RP80	
397			Dioxin (MOD)	C612A518
388			Educational Level	C632P001
375	Dioxin (MOD)	C612A518		
361			Compound Interest	*P610A515*
359			Weight History	C660P004
357			Wine	P623A618
354	Educational Level	C632P001		
349			Package	C657P001
348	Compound Interest	*P610A515*		
343			Cooper Test Amoeba	C665P002 C641P001
341	Wine	P623A618		
335			BMI	C624A620
334			Study Fees	C661P002
333			Inflation	C620A612
332	Weight History	C660P004		
331			Peanuts	C634P002
330			NZ Exports	C644P002
328			Fertilizer	C651P002
327			Classified	C622A615
326	Cooper Test	C665P002		
324	Amoeba	C641P001	Study Fees Peanuts Orchestra Tickets	C661P001 C664P001 C634P001
323			Map	C617A605
322			Temp Scale	C611A517
320	BMI	C624A620		
319			Six Pack 1 Lab Report	C618A608 C636P001
318	Peanuts	C634P002		
317	NZ Exports	C644P002		
315	Study Fees Package	C661P002 C657P001	Map	C617A606
314	Fertilizer	C651P002		
308	Study Fees	C661P001		
308	Inflation	C620A612		
307	Orchestra Tickets	C664P001		
305	Peanuts	C634P001		
303	Map	C617A605		
302			Tiles	C619A609
301	Classified	C622A615		
299			Weight History Tree	C660P003 C608A513
297	Six Pack 1	C618A608		
296	Temp Scale	C611A517		
294	Lab Report	C636P001	Solution	C606A509
292			Wine	C623A617
289			Educational Level	C632P002
287	Map	C617A606	Urban Population	C650P001
285			Temp Scale	C611A516
284			Photo	C605A506
283			Inflation	C620A610
282	Tiles	C619A609	Wine	C623A616
280			Price Tag Rope	C602A503 *P666P001*
278			Rug Production	C646P002
277				
276	Wine Weight history	C623A617 C660P003		
273	Solution	C606A509		
271			PriceTag	C602A502
270			Logbook	C613A520
267	Inflation	C620A610		
267			Path	C655P001
266	Educational Level	C632P002		
263			Airport Timetable	C645P001
262			Photo	C605A507
261	Temp Scale	C611A516		
260	Urban Population Tree	C650P001 C608A513	TV	C607A510
259	Photo Price Tag	C605A506 C602A503		
258	Wine	C623A616	Cooper Test	C665P001
256	Rug Production	C646P002		
255			Candles	C615A603
252			Gas Gauge	C604A505
250	Logbook	C613A520	BMI Candles	C624A619 C615A602

...

[Part 2/2]

Table A.2 **Location of items on the numeracy scale using RP67 and RP80**

Score	RP67		RP80	
249	Path	C655P001	Photo Six Pack 1	C605A508 C618A607
242	Photo	C605A507		
240	Rope	P666P001		
239	TV	C607A510		
238	Price Tag	C602A502		
234	Cooper Test	C665P001		
231	Candles Airport Timetable	C615A603 C645P001		
228	Gas Gauge	C604A505		
227	Photo	C605A508		
221	BMI Candles	C624A619 C615A602		
219			Odometer	P640P001
217	Six Pack 1	C618A607		
212			Watch	C614A601
201			Price Tag	C602A501
200			Parking Map	C635P001
195	Odometer	P640P001		
185	Watch	C614A601		
183			Election Results	C600AC04
179	Parking Map	C635P001		
168	Price Tag	C602A501		
167			Bottles	C601AC06
155	Election Results	C600AC04		
129	Bottles	C601AC06		

As the score point ranges defining the proficiency levels for literacy and numeracy have not changed between IALS and ALL and the Survey of Adult Skills, the group of items used to describe each proficiency level – i.e. those that are located in the score-point range that defines a proficiency level – changes. This necessitated revising the descriptors of the proficiency levels. Tables A.3 and A.4 present the descriptors used in the Survey of Adult Skills and the previous surveys.

[Part 1/2]

Table A.3 **Descriptors of literacy proficiency levels**

Level	Score range	Survey of Adult Skills (PIAAC) Literacy (RP67)	ALL/IALS Prose literacy (RP80)	ALL/IALS Document literacy (RP80)
1	Lower than 225	Most of the tasks at this level require the respondent to read relatively short digital or print continuous, non-continuous, or mixed texts to locate a single piece of information which is identical to or synonymous with the information given in the question or directive. Some tasks may require the respondent to enter personal information onto a document, in the case of some non-continuous texts. Little, if any, competing information is present. Some tasks may require simple cycling through more than one piece of information. Knowledge and skill in recognising basic vocabulary, evaluating the meaning of sentences, and reading of paragraph text is expected.	Most of the tasks at this level require the respondent to read relatively short text to locate a single piece of information which is identical to or synonymous with the information given in the question or directive. If plausible but incorrect information is present in the text, it tends not to be located near the correct information.	Tasks at this level tend to require the respondent either to locate a piece of information based on a literal match or to enter information from personal knowledge onto a document. Little, if any, distracting information is present.
2	226-275	At this level the complexity of text increases. The medium of texts may be digital or printed, and texts may be comprised of continuous, non-continuous, or mixed types. Tasks in this level require respondents to make matches between the text and information, and may require paraphrase or low-level inferences. Some competing pieces of information may be present. Some tasks require the respondent to: • cycle through or integrate two or more pieces of information based on criteria, • compare and contrast or reason about information requested in the question, or • navigate within digital texts to access-and-identify information from various parts of a document.	Some tasks at this level require respondents to locate a single piece of information in the text; however, several distractors or plausible but incorrect pieces of information may be present, or low-level inferences may be required. Other tasks require the respondent to integrate two or more pieces of information or to compare and contrast easily identifiable information based on a criterion provided in the question or directive.	Tasks at this level are more varied than those in Level 1. Some require the respondents to match a single piece of information; however, several distractors may be present, or the match may require low-level inferences. Tasks in this level may also ask the respondent to cycle through information in a document or to integrate information from various parts of a document.
3	276-325	Texts at this level are often dense or lengthy, including continuous, non-continuous, mixed, or multiple pages. Understanding text and rhetorical structures become more central to successfully completing tasks, especially in navigation of complex digital texts. Tasks require the respondent to identify, interpret, or evaluate one or more pieces of information, and often require varying levels of inference. Many tasks require the respondent construct meaning across larger chunks of text or perform multi-step operations in order to identify and formulate responses. Often tasks also demand that the respondent disregard irrelevant or inappropriate text content to answer accurately. Competing information is often present, but it is not more prominent than the correct information.	Tasks at this level tend to require respondents to make literal or synonymous matches between the text and information given in the task, or to make matches that require low-level inferences. Other tasks ask respondents to integrate information from dense or lengthy text that contains no organisational aids such as headings. Respondents may also be asked to generate a response based on information that can be easily identified in the text. Distracting information is present, but is not located near the correct information.	Some tasks at this level require the respondent to integrate multiple pieces of information from one or more documents. Others ask respondents to cycle through rather complex tables or graphs which contain information that is irrelevant or inappropriate to the task.

...

[Part 2/2]

Table A.3 **Descriptors of literacy proficiency levels**

Level	Score range	Survey of Adult Skills (PIAAC) Literacy (RP67)	ALL/IALS Prose literacy (RP80)	ALL/IALS Document literacy (RP80)
4	326-375	Tasks at this level often require respondents to perform multiple-step operations to integrate, interpret, or synthesise information from complex or lengthy continuous, non-continuous, mixed, or multiple type texts. Complex inferences and application of background knowledge may be needed to perform successfully. Many tasks require identifying and understanding one or more specific, non-central ideas in the text in order to interpret or evaluate subtle evidence-claim or persuasive discourse relationships. Conditional information is frequently present in tasks at this level and must be taken into consideration by the respondent. Competing information is present and sometimes seemingly as prominent as correct information.	These tasks require respondents to perform multiple-feature matches and to integrate or synthesise information from complex or lengthy passages. More complex inferences are needed to perform successfully. Conditional information is frequently present in tasks at this level and must be taken into consideration by the respondent.	Tasks at this level, like those at the previous levels, ask respondents to perform multiple-feature matches, cycle through documents, and integrate information; however, they require a greater degree of inference. Many of these tasks require respondents to provide numerous responses but do not designate how many responses are needed. Conditional information is also present in the document tasks at this level and must be taken into account by the respondent.
5	Higher than 376	At this level, tasks may require the respondent to search for and integrate information across multiple, dense texts; construct syntheses of similar and contrasting ideas or points of view; or evaluate evidenced based arguments. Application and evaluation of logical and conceptual models of ideas may be required to accomplish tasks. Evaluating reliability of evidentiary sources and selecting key information is frequently a key requirement. Tasks often require respondents to be aware of subtle, rhetorical cues and to make high-level inferences or use specialised background knowledge.	Some tasks at this level require the respondent to search for information in dense text which contains a number of plausible distractors. Others ask respondents to make high-level inferences or use specialised background knowledge. Some tasks ask respondents to contrast complex information.	Tasks at this level require the respondent to search through complex displays that contain multiple distractors, to make high-level text-based inferences, and to use specialised knowledge.

Table A.4 **Descriptors of literacy proficiency levels**

Level	Score range	Survey of Adult Skills (PIAAC) (RP67)	ALL (RP80)
1	Lower than 225	Tasks at this level require the respondent to carry out basic mathematical processes in common, concrete contexts where the mathematical content is explicit with little text and minimal distractors. Tasks usually require one-step or simple processes involving e.g. counting, sorting, performing basic arithmetic operations, understanding simple percentages such as 50%, locating and identifying elements of simple or common graphical or spatial representations.	Tasks at this level require the respondent to show an understanding of basic numerical ideas by completing simple tasks in concrete, familiar contexts where the mathematical content is explicit with little text. Tasks consist of simple, one-step operations such as counting, sorting dates, performing simple arithmetic operations or understanding common and simple percentages such as 50%.
2	226-275	Tasks at this level require the respondent to identify and act upon mathematical information and ideas embedded in a range of common contexts where the mathematical content is fairly explicit or visual with relatively few distractors. Tasks tend to require the application of two or more steps or processes involving e.g. calculation with whole numbers and common decimals, percentages and fractions; simple measurement and spatial representation; estimation; and interpretation of relatively simple data and statistics in texts, tables and graphs.	Tasks at this level are fairly simple and relate to identifying and understanding basic mathematical concepts embedded in a range of familiar contexts where the mathematical content is quite explicit and visual with few distractors. Tasks tend to include one-step or two-step processes and estimations involving whole numbers, benchmark percentages and fractions, interpreting simple graphical or spatial representations, and performing simple measurements.
3	276-325	Tasks at this level require the respondent to understand mathematical information which may be less explicit, embedded in contexts that are not always familiar and represented in more complex ways. Tasks require several steps and may involve the choice of problem-solving strategies and relevant processes. Tasks tend to require the application of e.g. number sense and spatial sense; recognising and working with mathematical relationships, patterns, and proportions expressed in verbal or numerical form; and interpretation and basic analysis of data and statistics in texts, tables and graphs.	Tasks at this level require the respondent to demonstrate understanding of mathematical information represented in a range of different forms, such as in numbers, symbols, maps, graphs, texts, and drawings. Skills required involve number and spatial sense, knowledge of mathematical patterns and relationships and the ability to interpret proportions, data and statistics embedded in relatively simple texts where there may be distractors. Tasks commonly involve undertaking a number of processes to solve problems.
4	326-375	Tasks at this level require the respondent to understand a broad range of mathematical information that may be complex, abstract or embedded in unfamiliar contexts. These tasks involve undertaking multiple steps and choosing relevant problem-solving strategies and processes. Tasks tend to require analysis and more complex reasoning about e.g. quantities and data; statistics and chance; spatial relationships; and change, proportions and formulas. Tasks at this level may also require comprehending arguments or communicating well-reasoned explanations for answers or choices.	Tasks at this level require respondents to understand a broad range of mathematical information of a more abstract nature represented in diverse ways, including in texts of increasing complexity or in unfamiliar contexts. These tasks involve undertaking multiple steps to find solutions to problems and require more complex reasoning and interpretation skills, including comprehending and working with proportions and formulas or offering explanations for answers.
5	Higher than 376	Tasks at this level require the respondent to understand complex representations and abstract and formal mathematical and statistical ideas, possibly embedded in complex texts. Respondents may have to integrate multiple types of mathematical information where considerable translation or interpretation is required; draw inferences; develop or work with mathematical arguments or models; justify, evaluate and critically reflect upon solutions or choices.	Tasks at this level require respondents to understand complex representations and abstract and formal mathematical and statistical ideas, possibly embedded in complex texts. Respondents may have to integrate multiple types of mathematical information, draw inferences, or generate mathematical justification for answers.

Source (IALS/ALL): OECD/Statistics Canada (2011).

References

OECD (2010), *PISA 2009 Results: What Students Know and Can Do: Student Performance in Reading, Mathematics and Science (Volume I)*, OECD Publishing, Paris, http://dx.doi.org/10.1787/9789264091450-en.

OECD/Statistics Canada (2011), *Literacy for Life: Further Results from the Adult Literacy and Life Skills Survey*, OECD Publishing, Paris, http://dx.doi.org/10.1787/9789264091269-en.

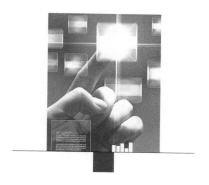

Annex B

Content of background questionnaires in the Survey of Adult Skills (PIAAC) and other skills surveys

Table B.1 **Summary of the background variables common to the Survey of Adult Skills (PIAAC), IALS and ALL**

Variable	Survey of Adult Skills (PIAAC)	International Adult Literacy Survey (IALS)	Adult Literacy and Life Skills Survey (ALL)
Demographics			
Age	X	X	X
Gender	X	X	X
Origin			
Born outside country	X	X	X
Country of birth	X	X	X
Age at which immigrated	X	X	X
Educational background			
Years of schooling	X	X	X
Highest level of educational attainment	X	X	X
Age at which highest qualification was completed	X		X
Language background			
First language learned	X	X	X
Language spoken most often at home	X	X	X
Social background			
Mother or female guardian born in another country	X	X	X
Highest level of education of mother or female guardian	X	X	X
Father or male guardian born in another country	X	X	X
Highest level of education of father or male guardian	X	X	X
Activity status and employment			
Activity status	X	X	X
Had paid work in previous 12 months	X	X	X
Occupation	X	X	X
Supervisory responsibilities			
Usual weekly hours of work in main job or business	X	X	X
Gross yearly earnings from employment	X	X	X
Gross yearly earnings from business	X	X	X
Skill use at work (target population: persons currently working or had worked in the previous 12 months)			
Reading activities in current or last job	X	X	X
Education or training in previous 12 months			
Undertook any education or training	X	X	X
Currently studying for a formal qualification	X	X	X
Reason for study is job-related	X		X
Participated in non-formal education or training in previous 12 months	X		X
Any learning activities in which respondent wanted to undertake but did not	X	X	X
Literacy and numeracy in everyday life			
Reading activities in everyday life	X	X	X
Health status			
Self-assessed health	X		X
Computer use			
Ever used a computer	X		X
Household			
Number of persons in household	X	X	X

Annex C

Project participants in Round 1 of the Survey of Adult Skills

INTERNATIONAL CONSORTIUM

Educational Testing Service (ETS) – *Overall Management, Test Development, Psychometrics, Analysis and Data Products*

Irwin Kirsch (International Project Director)
Claudia Tamassia (International Project Manager)
Kentaro Yamamoto (Director, Psychometrics and Analysis)
Matthias von Davier (Co-Director, Psychometrics and Analysis)
Marylou Lennon (Test Development, Literacy and PSTRE)
John P. Sabatini (Test Development, Reading Components)
Kelly M. Bruce (Test Development, Reading Components)
Eugenio Gonzalez (Training and Technical Report)
Michael Wagner (Director, Platform Development)
Larry Hanover (Editorial Support)
Judy Mendez (Project Support)
Lisa Hemat (Project Support)
Jason Bonthron (Platform Development)
Mike Ecker (Platform Development)
Ramin Hemat (Platform Development)
Tom Florek (Platform Development)
Debbie Pisacreta (Platform Development)
Janet Stumper (Platform Development)
John Barone (Director, Data Analysis and Database Preparation)
Scott Davis (Data Analysis)
Justin Herbert (Data Analysis)
Steven Holtzman (Data Analysis)
Laura Jerry (Data Analysis)
Mathew Kandathil (Data Analysis Leader)
Debra Kline (Data Management)
Nan Kong (Data Analysis)
Phillip Leung (Data Analysis Leader)
Chen Li (Data Analysis)
Mei-Jang Lin (Data Analysis)
Michael Narcowich (Data Analysis)
Alfred Rogers (Data Analysis Leader)
Jonathan Steinberg (Data Analysis)
Joan Stoeckel (Data Analysis and Data Management)
Ruopei Sun (Data Analysis)
Minhwei Wang (Data Analysis Leader)
Kei Sing Wong (Data Analysis)
Lingjun Wong (Data Analysis)
Jeffrey Wright (Data Analysis)
Fred Yan (Data Analysis)
Ningshan Zhang (Data Analysis)
Danielle Baum (Consultant, Paper Booklets)
Juliette Mendelovits (Consultant, Literacy Test Development, ACER)
Dara Searle (Consultant, Literacy Test Development, ACER)

GESIS – *Development of the Job Requirement Approach Module and Background Questionnaire*

Beatrice Rammstedt (Lead)
Dorothée Behr
Susanne Helmschrott
Silke Martin
Natascha Massing
Anouk Zabal

Deutsches Institut für Internationale Pädagogische Forschung (DIPF) – *Development of the PIAAC Test Delivery Platform*

Ingo Barkow (International IT Support)
Robert Baumann (Software Development)
Simon Brüchner (Software Development)
Mahtab Dalir (Software Development)
Alexander During (Software Development)
Gabriele Gissler (Item Development)
Frank Goldhammer (Test Development, Deputy Project Co-Director)
Roland Johannes (Software Development)
Elham Müller (Software Development)
Jean-Paul Reeff (International Consultant)
Marc Rittberger (Director)
Heiko Rölke (Project Co-Director)
Maya Schnitzler (Software Development)
Felix Toth (Software Development)
Britta Upsing (Project Co-ordinator)

cApStAn – *Linguistic Quality Control*

Steve Dept (Verification Operations)
Andrea Ferrari (Verification Methodology and Management)
Laura Wäyrynen (Verification Methodology and Management)
Elica Krajčeva (Verification Management)
Raphaël Choppinet (Verification Management)
Shinoh Lee (Verification Management)
Irene Liberati (Verification Management)

Research Centre for Education and the Labour Market (ROA), Maastricht University – *Development of the Job Requirement Approach Module and Background Questionnaire*

Rolf van der Velden (Co-ordinator, Background Questionnaire Development)
Jim Allen (Background Questionnaire Development)
Martin Humburg (Background Questionnaire Development)

International Association for the Evaluation of Educational Achievement (IEA) – *Data Cleaning and Database Preparation*

Alena Becker (Data Processing and National Adaptations)
Christine Busch (Meta-data and Processing)
Ralph Carstens (Lead International Data Management and Analysis Support/Training)
Mark Cockle (Quality Control and Manuals)
Tim Daniel (Co-Lead International Data Management)
Bastian Deppe (Software Testing and Data Cleaning)
Limiao Duan (Processing Systems Development)
Daniela Tranziska (Processing Systems Development)
Christian Harries (Software Development)
Pamela Inostroza (Processing Systems Development)
Matthias Jenzen (Software Development)
Maike Junod (Software Development)

Alexander Konn (Processing Systems Development)

Kamil Kowolik (Data Processing and National Adaptations)

Alexander Lebedev (Software Testing)

Sebastian Meyer (Data Processing and National Adaptations)

Pia Möbus (Software Testing and Data Cleaning)

Jirka Neumann (Data Processing and National Adaptations)

Brice Nzuakue Diogni (Software Testing)

Dirk Oehler (Quality Control and Processing Systems)

Martin Olszewski (Processing Systems Testing)

Daniel Radtke (Data Processing and National Adaptations)

Frank Wohnfurter (Software Development)

Westat – *Sample Design and Selection, Weighting, Survey Operations, and Quality Control*

Leyla Mohadjer (Director, Sampling Activities)

Pat Montalvan (Director, Survey Operations)

Tom Krenzke (Manager, Sampling Activities)

Michael Lemay (Manager, Survey Operations)

Wendy Van de Kerckhove (Senior Leader, Sampling Activities)

Valerie Hsu (Leader, Sampling Activities)

Laura Alvarez-Rojas (Senior Survey Statistician)

Lillian Diaz-Hoffmann (Survey Operations Material Development and Training)

Sylvia Dohrmann (Senior Survey Statistician)

Jarrod Grebing (Survey Operations Training)

Hongsheng Hao (Senior Survey Statistician)

Wen-Chau Haung (Senior Systems Analyst)

Michael Jones (Senior Survey Statistician)

Robin Jones (Senior Systems Analyst)

Jane Li (Senior Survey Statistician)

Lin Li (Senior Survey Statistician)

Yuki Nakamoto (Senior Systems Analyst)

Margo Tercy (Project Support)

Klaus Teuter (Senior Systems Analyst)

Chao Zhou (Survey Statistician)

Public Research Center Henri Tudor – *Development of the Computer-Based Platform for the Background Questionnaire*

Thibaud Latour (Scientific Unit Leader, Project Co-ordination)

Isabelle Jars (Project Management)

Raynald Jadoul (Software Architecture and Staff Co-ordination)

Patrick Plichart (Platform Architecture)

Vincent Porro (Lead Designer and Development)

Lionel Lecaque (Platform Integration)

Jérôme Bogaerts (Lead Developer)

Joël Billard (Questionnaire Development)

Damien Arcani (Contents Designer)

Somsack Sipasseuth (Workflow Development)

Primaël Lorbat (Multilingual Framework Development)

Younes Djaghloul (Multilingual Framework Development)

Igor Ribassin (Virtual Machine Integration)

Pierre Goulaieff (Communication)

EXPERT GROUPS

PIAAC Background Questionnaire Expert Group

Ken Mayhew (Chair), Pembroke College, Oxford and SKOPE, Research Centre on Skills, Knowledge and Organisational Performance, United Kingdom

Patrice de Broucker, Statistics Canada, Canada

Enrique Fernandez, European Foundation for the Improvement of Living and Working Conditions, Ireland

Masako Kurosawa, National Graduate Institute for Policy Studies, Japan

Kea Tijdens, University of Amsterdam, Netherlands

Scott Murray, Canada

Jürgen Schupp, The Free University of Berlin and the German Institute for Economic Research DIW, Germany

Tom W. Smith, University of Chicago, United States

Robert Willis, Population Studies Center, University of Michigan, United States

PIAAC Literacy Expert Group

Stan Jones (Chair), Canada

Egil Gabrielsen, Center for Reading Research, University of Stavanger, Norway

Jan Hagston, Australia

Pirjo Linnakylä, University of Jyväskylä, Finland

Hakima Megherbi, University of Paris, France

John Sabatini, Educational Testing Service, United States

Monika Tröster, German Institute for Adult Education, Germany

Eduardo Vidal-Abarca, Department of Psychology, University of Valencia, Spain

PIAAC Numeracy Expert Group

Iddo Gal (Chair), University of Haifa, Israel

Silvia Alatorre, National Pedagogical University, Mexico

Sean Close, St. Patrick's College, Ireland

Jeff Evans, Middlesex University, United Kingdom

Lene Johansen, Aalborg University, Denmark

Terry Maguire, Institute of Technology Tallaght-Dublin, Ireland

Myrna Manly, United States

Dave Tout, Australian Council for Educational Research, Australia

PIAAC Problem Solving in Technology-Rich Environments Expert Group

Jean-François Rouet (Chair), CNRS and University of Poitiers, France

Mirelle Bétrancourt, University of Geneva, Switzerland

Anne Britt, Northern Illinois University, United States

Rainer Bromme, University of Muenster, Germany

Arthur C. Graesser, University of Memphis, United States

Jonna M. Kulikowich, Pennsylvania State University, United States

Donald J. Leu, University of Connecticut, United States

Naoki Ueno, Musashi Institute of Technology, Japan

Herre van Oostendorp, Utrecht University, the Netherlands

Reading Components Expert Group

John P. Sabatini, Educational Testing Service, United States

Kelly M. Bruce, Educational Testing Service, United States

Technical Advisory Group

Cees A. W. Glas (Chair), Institute for Behavioural Research at the University of Twente, Netherlands

Roel J. Bosker, Groningen Institute for Educational Research at the University of Groningen, Netherlands

Henry Braun, Boston College, United States

Lars Lyberg, Sweden

Robert J. Mislevy, Education Testing Service and University of Maryland, United States

Christian Monseur, University of Liege, Belgium

Irini Moustaki, London School of Economics, and Athens University of Economics and Business, United Kingdom and Greece

BOARD OF PARTICIPATING COUNTRIES

Co-Chairs

Satya Brink (Canada) (2008-10)

Dan McGrath (United States) (2010-13)

Paolo Sestito (Italy) (2008-13)

Delegates

Australia: Paul Cmiel, Shannon Madden, Scott Matheson and Mark Roddam

Austria: Helmut Höpflinger (2008-09), Robert Jellasitz (from 2009), Mark Német

Belgium (Flanders): Raf Boey and Anton Derks

Canada: Satya Brink, Patrick Bussière, Mark Hopkins, Barbara Leung, Valerie Saysset, Katerina Sukovski and Allen Sutherland

Czech Republic: Petr Mateju (2008-11) Jakub Starek (from Jan 2011)

Denmark: Jan Reitz Jørgensen, Michael Justesen (2008-12) and Ditte Sølvhøj (from May 2012)

Estonia: Tiina Annus

Finland: Jorma Ahola (2008-10), Petri Haltia, Ville Heinonen, Reijo Laukkanen, Petra Packalén and Varpu Weijola

France: Patrick Pommier

Germany: Andreas Henkes and Alexander Renner

Ireland: Pat Hayden, Seamus Hempenstall (2008-13) and Majella O'Dea (from Feb. 2013)

Italy: Gabriella Di Francesco, Alessandra Tomai and Andrea Valenti

Japan: Ryo Watanabe

Korea: Sooyoung Lee and Eon Lim

Netherlands: Maurice Doll (from 2012), Geralt Nekkers (2008-11) and Ted Reininga

Norway: Lars Nerdrum, Sverre Try and Gry Høeg Ulverud

Poland: Lidia Olak

Slovak Republic: Júlia Štepánková

Spain: Sagrario Avezuela Sánchez, Jesús Barroso Barrero (from 2012), Adolfo Hernández Gordillo, Enrique Roca Cobo (until 2012) and Ismael Sanz Labrador

Sweden: Dan Grannas (from 2010), Helen Kaplan (2008-10), Carina Lindén and Nina Waldenström (2008-10)

United Kingdom: Anthony Clarke, Euan Dick and Stephen Leman

United States: Melvin Brodsky and Daniel McGrath

European Commission: Anastasios Bisopoulos and Jens Fischer-Kottenstede

NATIONAL PROJECT MANAGERS

Australia: Loucas Harous, Cynthia Millar, Theo Neumann and Wendy Ozols

Austria: Markus Bönisch and Eduard Stöger

Belgium (Flanders): Inge de Meyer

Canada: Sylvie Grenier

Cyprus[1]: Athena Michaelidou

Czech Republic: Jana Strakova

Denmark: Torben Friberg and Anders Rosdahl

Estonia: Vivika Halapuu and Aune Valk

Finland: Pirjo Linnakylä and Antero Malin

France: Arnaud Degorre (from 2008 to Aug. 2009) and Nicolas Jonas (from Sept. 2009)

Germany: Beatrice Rammstedt

Ireland: Donal Kelly

Italy: Manuela Amendola, Michela Bastianelli, Gabriella Di Francesco; Vittoria Gallina, Simona Mineo and Fabio Roma

Japan: Atsushi Kogirima and Daisuke Machida

Korea: Sooyoung Lee and Eon Lim

Netherlands: Willem Houtkoop and Marieke Buisman

Norway: Birgit Bjørkeng, Vibeke Opheim, Elisabeth Rønning and Nils Vibe

Poland: Jan Burski (from May 2012), Michał Federowicz, Artur Pokropek and Mateusz Żółtak (until April 2012)

Russian Federation: Oleg Podolskiy and Dmitry Popov

Slovak Republic: Zuzana Lukackova (until April 2011), Adriana Mesarosova (from April 2011), Ildiko Pathoova

Spain: Rosario Álvarez Vara (until Sept. 2009), Azucena Corredera González (from Sept. 2009 to Sept. 2011), Angeles Picado Vallés (from Sept. 2011 to Sept. 2012), Inés Sancha Gonzalo (from Sept. 2009) and Luis Sanz San Miguel (from Sept. 2012)

Sweden: Ann-Charlott Larsson

United Kingdom: Anthony Clarke, Julie Sewell and Rebecca Wheater

United States: Eugene Owen and Stephen Provasnik

. . . .

1. See notes at the end of this Annex.

OECD SECRETARIAT

Veronica Borg, Consultant, (2013)

Fionnuala Canning, Project Assistant (2008-11)

Ji Eun Chung, Analyst (2012-13)

Niccolina Clements, Project Assistant (2010-11)

Vanessa Denis, Statistician (2012-13)

Richard Desjardins, Analyst (2010-13)

Marta Encinas-Martin, Analyst (2012-13)

Anne Fichen, Statistician (2013)

Paulina Granados Zambrano, Statistician (2012-13)

Bo Hansson, Analyst, (2008-09)

Mark Keese, Head of Division (2008-13)

Viktoria Kis, Analyst (2012-13)

Sabrina Leonarduzzi, Project Assistant (2010-13)

Alistair Nolan, Senior Economist (2004-07)

Michele Pellizzari, Analyst (2012-13)

Glenda Quintini, Senior Analyst (2011-13)

Yasuhito Sakurai, Analyst (2010-13)

Andreas Schleicher, Deputy Director, strategic development and co-ordination (2008-13)

Takashi Sukegawa, Analyst (2009-10)

William Thorn, Senior Analyst and Project Manager (2008-13)

Annex D

**Project participants in Round 2
of the Survey of Adult Skills**

INTERNATIONAL CONSORTIUM

Educational Testing Service (ETS) – *Overall Management, Test Development, Psychometrics, Analysis and Data Products*

Irwin Kirsch (International Project Director)

Claudia Tamassia (International Project Manager)

Kentaro Yamamoto (Director, Psychometrics and Analysis)

Matthias von Davier (Co-Director, Psychometrics and Analysis)

Michael Wagner (Director, Platform Development)

Marylou Lennon (Test Development, Literacy and PSTRE)

John P. Sabatini (Test Development, Reading Components)

Kelly M. Bruce (Test Development, Reading Components)

Lale Khorramdel (Psychometrics and Analysis)

Jon Weeks (Psychometrics and Analysis)

Henry Chen (Psychometrics and Analysis)

Chentong Chen (Psychometrics and Analysis)

Eugenio Gonzalez (Training, Technical Report and Data Products)

Isabelle Jars (Project Management)

Larry Hanover (Editorial Support)

Judy Mendez (Project Support)

Lisa Hemat (Project Support)

Jason Bonthron (Platform Development)

Ramin Hemat (Platform Development)

Chris Nicoletti (Platform Development)

John Barone (Director, Data Analysis and Database Preparation)

Kevin Bentley (Data Products)

Karen Castellano (Data Analysis)

Scott Davis (Data Analysis)

Mary Beth Hanly (Data Products)

Steven Holtzman (Data Analysis)

Laura Jerry (Data Analysis)

Mathew Kandathil (Data Analysis Leader)

Lokesh Kapur (Data Analysis)

Debra Kline (Data Management)

Phillip Leung (Data Analysis Leader)

Mei-Jang Lin (Data Analysis)

Alfred Rogers (Data Analysis Leader)

Ruopei Sun (Data Analysis)

Carla Tarsitano (Data Management)

Sarah Venema (Data Products)

Minhwei Wang (Data Analysis Leader)

Lingjun Wong (Data Analysis)

Jeffrey Wright (Data Analysis)

Wei Zhao (Data Analysis)

Jun Xu (Data Analysis)

GESIS – *Development of the Job Requirement Approach Module and Background Questionnaire*

Beatrice Rammstedt (Lead)

Dorothée Behr

Natascha Massing

Anouk Zabal

Deutsches Institut für Internationale Pädagogische Forschung (DIPF) – *Development of the PIAAC Test Delivery Platform*

Ingo Barkow (International IT Support)

Robert Baumann (Software Development)

Mahtab Dalir (Software Development)

Frank Goldhammer (Deputy Project Co-Director)

Sabrina Hermann (Project Coordinator)

Roland Johannes (Software Development, International Co-ITC)

Jean-Paul Reeff (International Consultant)

Marc Rittberger (Director)

Heiko Rölke (Project Co-Director)

Britta Upsing (Project Coordinator)

Carolin Ziegler (Project Coordinator)

cApStAn – *Linguistic Quality Control*

Steve Dept (Verification Operations)

Andrea Ferrari (Verification Methodology and Management)

Laura Wäyrynen (Verification Methodology and Management)

Elica Krajčeva (Verification Management)

Shinoh Lee (Verification Management)

Irene Liberati (Verification Management)

Research Centre for Education and the Labour Market (ROA), Maastricht University – *Development of the Job Requirement Approach Module and Background Questionnaire*

Rolf van der Velden (Coordinator, Development Background Questionnaire)

Jim Allen (Development Background Questionnaire)

Martin Humburg (Development Background Questionnaire)

Mark Levels (Development Background Questionnaire)

International Association for the Evaluation of Educational Achievement (IEA) – *Data Cleaning and Database Preparation*

Alena Becker (Data Processing and National Adaptations)

Christine Busch (Meta-data and Processing)

Ralph Carstens (Lead International Data Management and Analysis Support/Training)

Tim Daniel (Lead International Data Management)

Limiao Duan (Processing Systems Development)

Christian Harries (Software Development)

Maike Junod (Software Development)

Hannah Köhler (Deputy Lead International Data Management)

Kamil Kowolik (Data Processing and National Adaptations)

Kathrin Krämer (Software Development)

Dirk Oehler (Quality Control and Processing Systems)

Liisa Vaht (Quality Control)

Svetoslav Velkov (Data Processing)

Westat – *Sample Design and Selection, Weighting, Survey Operations, and Quality Control*

Leyla Mohadjer (Director, Sampling Activities)

Pat Montalvan (Director, Survey Operations)

Jacquie Hogan (Survey Operations Training)

Tom Krenzke (Manager, Sampling Activities)

Michael Lemay (Manager, Survey Operations)

Wendy Van de Kerckhove (Senior Leader, Sampling Activities)

Valerie Hsu (Leader, Sampling Activities)

Lin Li (Leader, Sampling Activities)

Jane Li (Senior Survey Statistician)

John Lopdell (Senior Survey Statistician)

Laura Alvarez-Rojas (Senior Survey Statistician)

Nina Thornton (Survey Operations Material Development and Training)

Baifan Li (Senior Systems Analyst)

Klaus Teuter (Senior Systems Analyst)

Luxembourg Institute for Science and Technology – Development of the Computer-Based Platform for the Background Questionnaire and Cognitive Assessment

Anne Hendrick (Platform Leader, Project Co-ordination)

Raynald Jadoul (Project Management and Software Architecture)

Vincent Porro (Lead Designer and Staff Co-ordination)

Primaël Lorbat (Multilingual Framework and Questionnaire Development)

Cédric Alfonsi (Portal Integration and Translation Support)

Somsack Sipasseuth (Workflow Development)

Igor Ribassin (Virtual Machine Integration)

Christophe Henry (System Integration)

Cyril Hazotte (System Administration)

EXPERT GROUPS

PIAAC Round 2 Technical Advisory Group

Cees A. W. Glas (Chair), University of Twente, the Netherlands

Henry Braun, Boston College, United States of America

Lars Lyberg, Stockholm University, Sweden

Irini Moustaki, London School of Economics, the United Kingdom

BOARD OF PARTICIPATING COUNTRIES

Co-Chairs

Aviana Bulgarelli (Italy) (2016)

Patrick Bussière (Canada) (2014-15)

Dan McGrath (United States) (2010-16)

Paolo Sestito (Italy) (2008-13)

Delegates

Chile: Francisco Meneses Ponzini (until Feb. 2016); Roberto Schurch (from Feb. 2016)

Greece: Magda Trantallidi

Indonesia: Linda Doortje Gonggalang (until March 2016); Yulia Naelufara (from March 2016)

Israel: Dmitri Romanov

Lithuania: Saulius Zybartas

New Zealand: David Earle (until March 2016); Nita Zodgekar (from March 2016)

Singapore: Soon Joo Gog

Slovenia: Ales Ojstersek

Turkey: Murat Aksoy

NATIONAL PROJECT MANAGERS

Chile: María Paola Sevilla Buitron (until Aug. 2013); Maria Francisca Donoso (from Oct. 2013)

Greece: Andromachi Hadjiyanni

Indonesia: Hari Setiadi

Israel: Zvika Amir

Lithuania: Viktorija Šeikienė (until Jan. 2013); Mindaugas Stundža (from Jan. to Aug. 2013); Sigita Uksaitė (from Aug. 2013 to June 2015)

New Zealand: Jit Cheung and Paul Satherley (jointly until April 2014); Paul Satherley (from May 2014)

Singapore: Emily Low

Slovenia: Sabina Melavc (until Jan. 2013); Estera Mozina (from Feb. 2013)

Turkey: Ercüment Işik (2012); Cengiz Aydemir (from Jan. 2013 to June 2015); Murat Aksoy from June 2015 to April 2016); Uğur Güneş (from April 2016)

OECD SECRETARIAT

Ji Eun Chung (Analyst)

Vanessa Denis (Statistician)

Marta Encinas-Martin (Analyst)

Paulina Granados Zambrano (Statistician)

Miloš Kankaraš (Analyst)

François Keslair (Statistician)

Sabrina Leonarduzzi (Project Assistant)

Guillermo Montt (Analyst)

Marco Paccagnella (Analyst)

Glenda Quintini (Senior Economist)

William Thorn (Senior Analyst and Project Manager)